SENSATION

SENSATION

The New Science
of Physical Intelligence

Thalma Lobel

ICON

Originally published in the USA in 2014 by Atria Books,
an imprint of Simon & Schuster Inc.

First published in the UK in 2014 by
Icon Books Ltd, Omnibus Business Centre,
39–41 North Road, London N7 9DP
email: info@iconbooks.net
www.iconbooks.net

Sold in the UK, Europe and Asia
by Faber & Faber Ltd, Bloomsbury House,
74–77 Great Russell Street,
London WC1B 3DA or their agents

Distributed in the UK, Europe and Asia
by TBS Ltd, TBS Distribution Centre, Colchester Road,
Frating Green, Colchester CO7 7DW

Distributed in South Africa by
Jonathan Ball, Office B4, The District,
41 Sir Lowry Road, Woodstock 7925

ISBN: 978-184831-659-1

Interior design by Jill Putorti

Printed and bound in the UK by
Clays Ltd, St Ives plc

To my beloved son Dani
To my beautiful Danielle, Elinor, Natalie and Dean

Contents

Introduction:
The Tangled Web Our Senses Weave

In 2005 I travelled with four friends to Guatemala for two weeks. In a great trip filled with many exciting new experiences, the highlight was a visit to Tikal National Park to see archaeological sites dating back to the Mayan civilisation.

In the jungle cottages where we stayed, each of us was given a separate room. My husband was not able to travel with me, so I was alone in the room. There was no electricity from 10.00 p.m. until the morning. Unable to sleep soundly, I awoke at 2.00 a.m. – to utter and total darkness. It was pitch-black. I had no flashlight or cell phone next to my bed, and I saw nothing. Nothing! No distant street lamp, no moonlight, not a star through the window. I could not hear anything either – the jungle around me was completely still. This was the closest I had ever been to sensory deprivation. It was a most unpleasant experience.

At dawn's first light, I got dressed and ran outside. With the sun on my face, hearing the chatter of birds, I felt reborn! No other person was in sight, but I revelled in the beauty and colours of nature and was delighted when a group of armadillos, an animal I had never before seen, ambled by. I was so grateful that life was not as barren and blank as it had seemed in that dark room. In those brief hours of darkness, I had come to realise, in the most emphatic way, the vital connection between our physical senses and our mental states.

It is crucial for us to be able to sense the external world, but at the other extreme from sensory deprivation is sensory overload, which can come from living and working in a big city. The urban environment is relentless and bustling – scurrying pedestrians, aggressive drivers, lumbering trucks and choking exhaust, kamikaze bike messengers, splashy window displays, the unbroken skyline of hard-edged buildings, the screaming heat and densely packed bodies. I for one love cities like New York, Los Angeles and Tel Aviv, where I live, but sometimes even I need to get away from it all – just for a while. Unlike me, other people get agitated by too much stimulation and prefer quieter, more natural landscapes in the suburbs or countryside.

Between these two poles lies an entire spectrum of stimuli. Total sensory deprivation and stimulus bombardment are both bad for us. Yet wherever we are, we are constantly exposed to environmental stimuli and cues. We touch things that have different temperatures and textures, we smell good and bad odours, we see myriad colours, and we lift objects to sense their weight. We experience much of our world quite consciously through our senses. But without noticing it, we are also unconsciously influenced in the most amazing ways by the physical experiences our senses convey.

In this book, I will take you on a systematic tour of our senses and reveal how your sensory experience of the world influences the rational mind you believe you have, as well as the independent thoughts you believe you make. I'll explain why warm temperatures make us temporarily friendlier and the colour red causes us to perform more poorly on tests. I'll show that drawing close dots on a Cartesian graph makes us feel more emotionally close to others and that CVs fastened to heavy clipboards make a better, more professional impression. And I'll demonstrate why clean smells, like that of Windolene, promote cleaning behaviour, while showering before a test is more likely to lead to cheating. In case these statements sound impossible, I have to tell you that these findings have been proven repeatedly in lab experiments and published in some of the best peer-reviewed academic journals in the world. These astonishing facts actually point to a new way of understanding how our minds work. And *Sensation* presents these studies to you, the general reader, for the first time.

This book is about the way our sensations influence us. Unseen cues that surround us may cause us to lose sleep, fail a test and even fall in love. In the Hans Christian Andersen fairy tale 'The Princess and the Pea', only a princess is sensitive enough to feel a pea placed underneath twenty featherbeds and twenty mattresses. But in fact we are all extraordinarily sensitive to the stimuli in our environment. Like the princess, we may not always know what disturbs us under our radar, but we are nonetheless affected.

Many of the effects of these triggers are short-lived; they 'glow' ephemerally in the subconscious for a little while but don't change us permanently. Yet what is brief is not necessarily unimportant. Our actions under these triggers' influence can make a significant difference in our effectiveness in business meetings, classrooms and sports. They can affect how we feel on first dates and how we're perceived in an interview for a job. This book will raise your awareness of these triggers, or 'peas', and their effects – on both your own and others' thoughts and actions.

*   *   *

My research into effects of their environment on people began, basically, when I was eighteen years old and a soldier in the Israel Defence Forces, where I was stationed in a classified bunker several storeys below ground. I was in my first year at my university, studying psychology, and would work 48-hour shifts at the base so I could leave to attend class, where I would sit through lectures about the human mind under extreme conditions. With a slight sense of irony, I would then return to a metal cave to work without sleep for another two days straight. My life was basically an experiment.

At the base, we lived and worked under relentless fluorescent lights, breathing the same recycled air over and over. We napped in small pitch-black rooms, where, during most of my time underground, I lost track of day and night. Immersed in psychology at the university when I was above ground, I couldn't help but study every facial expression and odd behaviour of my fellow soldiers whenever I returned to the bunker. I didn't realise it at the time, but I was already fascinated by the way our environments shape and influence us. The world became a lab to me.

I received my degree in clinical psychology and followed it with postdoctoral studies at Harvard. As a professor of psychology, I studied how stereotypes, personality characteristics and culture influence our behaviour, specialising in the psychology of gender identity in both children and adults. I designed interesting experiments that were published in prestigious journals, and I truly loved what I did.

Then, in 2008, I read a study by Laurence Williams and John Bargh in *Science*.[1] They had found that subjects who held warm cups of coffee were more likely to perceive someone else as emotionally 'warm'. The results of this study, and others like it, seemed almost like science fiction in their revelation of subtle but profound influences on our thoughts, perceptions and judgements. They moved me in a way that no studies ever had before. Reading them reminded me of how, after reading a book about psychoanalysis as a senior in high school, I'd been thrilled to discover the power of the unconscious to influence our minds and bodies. The stories of patients who had suffered from physical symptoms such as paralysis or vision disturbances but were cured by 'talking techniques', by becoming aware of unconscious drives that caused their symptoms, had inspired me to become a psychologist. Now here was another kind of revolution in psychology.

But these studies were conducted in a lab, with regular people who did not suffer from any pathological maladies. These new studies examined everyday behaviours, such as interactions with friends, evaluations of job candidates and social judgements. Moreover, the studies did not deal with hidden or deeply suppressed motives, desires and fears that unconsciously influence our behaviour. Rather, they dealt with physical sensations that we experience all the time and that unconsciously influence our behaviours.

Most of us would like to believe that we exert control over our behaviour; so it is somewhat disconcerting to discover that seemingly irrelevant environmental factors and physical sensations affect our behaviour all the time. The findings were counter-intuitive – and so they were alluring to me. I decided to return to research into the association between body and mind, but with this new approach, which is now known as the theory of *embodied cognition*.

I'd grown up in busy Tel Aviv, but I used to spend summers with my aunt on her kibbutz, which gave me some of my best childhood memories. In those days, living on the kibbutz was like living on another planet – no phones, no cars, just endless fields with houses sprouting up here and there. People were different there, calmer; they even wore different expressions on their faces. Whenever I visited, I noticed that I was different too. We all felt part of a larger landscape and purpose; we were more in touch with the forces of nature and how they ruled our lives and routines. One summer there, I had an epiphany that we are more like sailing boats than motorboats; even though our hands are on the wheel, the unseen force of the wind matters much more than we do. Now, as an adult, after a lifetime of studying the mind, I finally have the science of embodied cognition to show that the little girl in a field was more right than she then knew.

Temperature, texture, weight, sound, taste, smell and colour, among a symphony of other physical sensations, affect us every day. We are moved without knowing we are being moved. We feel ownership of and responsibility for our decisions and actions, yet they are greatly influenced and sometimes created by the sensory world around us.

After 30 years of conducting my own studies, studying the research of others, and teaching thousands of students, I am more inspired than ever by this *embodied* material. When I teach my graduate students about these recent studies, I can see their surprise. And when my students and I create our own experiments, we surprise ourselves. Several studies, for example, found that people's moral judgements of others are affected by disgusting tastes. Yet I would venture to guess that you, like most people, feel that your moral values come from deep inner convictions that are unassailable by simple, transient changes in your environment.

I'll begin by discussing the effects of temperature on our moods and the decisions we make. It turns out there is reason behind why we sometimes blow hot and cold. I believe that you will be as fascinated as my students and I have been with these innovative experiments, the theories behind them, and their implications for your own life.

Wanna Grab a Drink?
How Temperature Affects Us

If you've ever been married, you know the rule: The husband is always to blame. My husband and I have been married for over thirty years and ten years ago decided to sell a small apartment that we owned in Tel Aviv. Although it was a beautiful, white-walled, sunny Bauhaus-style apartment in the city centre, it had become a hassle for us to manage. We had many potential buyers come and go, but one particular newly-wed couple kept coming to see it over and over again. On one visit, they even brought in an architect, who measured and fussed all over the place in a consultation about remodelling. They clearly wanted to buy.

We talked a little about numbers on their visits, but Israelis are notoriously coy negotiators, and we had made it nearly to the signing of the final paperwork without yet agreeing on the price. For what would be our last negotiation, we planned to meet the couple at a mutual friend's house to talk over tea. I remember clearly that on the way to that meeting, I believed their offer was too low and I planned to make a firm counter-offer. I practised in my head all the ways I would talk about the value of the apartment, its great location and other buyers' interest in it. After we arrived, our hosts poured us all hot cups of black tea, and within ten minutes I found that I had agreed to the buyers' original – and too low – offer.

When I came home, I was kicking myself, because I had the feeling that we could have easily gotten more if we had insisted. The couple was clearly very invested. Why had we given up so easily? Naturally, I decided it must have been my husband's fault. Why hadn't *he* argued? Why had we agreed so quickly? Maybe we had just gotten tired of the long negotiation and wanted to be done with it. Maybe we just liked the young couple. Years later, I found out that something far simpler was likely to have played a role: the warm cup of tea.

In 2008, at Yale University, a student named Laurence Williams and his well-known professor John Bargh recruited 41 students for a psychology study.[1] One by one, the students were led into a lobby, where they were greeted by a young research assistant who guided them to an elevator that would take them to a laboratory on the fourth floor. As part of the experiment, the assistant had her hands full, carrying a stack of books, a clipboard and a cup of coffee. While in the elevator, she asked the participant to hold her coffee for a second, so she could write his or her name and other information on her clipboard. This casual request was actually the most important part of the experimental procedure. Half of the participants were handed a hot cup of coffee and the other half an iced coffee. This subtly exposed them to different tactile experiences of temperature. Yet they had no idea that what they were being asked to do was significant.

When the participants stepped out of the elevator and into the lab, they were met by another experimenter, who sat them down and asked them to read a description of someone called only Person A, who was characterised as skilful, intelligent, determined, practical, industrious and cautious. Unbeknownst to the participants, Person A was a fictitious composite character. They were then asked to rate Person A from a list of ten additional traits not included in the written description. Half of the traits were on the 'warm–cold' spectrum – traits that we might associate with 'warm' or 'cold' personalities – and were identified by words such as *generous* or *ungenerous, good-natured* or *irritable, sociable* or *antisocial,* and *caring* or *selfish.* The remaining traits were unrelated to the warm–cold aspect and included descriptions such as *talkative* or *quiet, strong* or *weak, honest* or *dishonest.*

Behold the power of holding a warm cup of coffee. Participants who held the hot cup for a few moments in the elevator rated Person A as significantly more generous, good-natured and caring than did their iced coffee-holding counterparts. People who held the cold cup were far more likely to see Person A as ungenerous, irritable and selfish. Yet they all felt pretty much the same about adjectives unrelated to the warm–cold aspect, no matter which coffee the subjects held before they sat down.

Could the insignificant act of holding a warm cup of coffee in an elevator really make you see the people around you as nicer? What was going on here, psychologically speaking?

This finding that physical warmth promotes interpersonal warmth was so surprising that many scientists raised their eyebrows and asked if it could be true. Yet, as you will soon see, temperature influences our reactions to real people just as it affected participants' initial judgements of anonymous people they only read about. Temperature can even influence our perceptions of intimacy and connection.

Although individuals differ in how much they need intimacy and to what extent they are capable of it, intimacy is an essential component of most relationships. In 2009, two Dutch researchers explored whether temperature could affect how close people thought they were to others.[2] As in the coffee experiment, the researchers had participants hold warm or cold beverages. The experimenter asked each participant to hold a beverage for a few minutes while he was pretending to install a questionnaire on the computer.

The experimenter then took the beverages from the participants and asked them to think of a real person they knew and rate how close they were to that person. Participants who were holding a warm beverage perceived the person in mind as closer emotionally to them than did those who were holding a cold beverage. This is surprising because most of us believe that our most intimate connections are stable on a day-to-day basis – we don't expect them to be influenced by the temperature of the drink we hold.

Yet our minds do not exist in a vacuum, so our feelings and values can be affected by subtle influences around us. Seemingly irrelevant things that we process through our bodies and our physical senses do affect our states of mind, mostly without our awareness. The core theory of embodied cognition, the emergent field of psychology that we're exploring, states that there is an indissoluble link between our decision making and our sensory-motor experiences, such as touching a warm or cold object, and our behaviours, judgements and emotions.

Conventional psychology historically has been interested in what's going on *inside* people's heads and why they make the mistakes and choices that they do. Psychologists usually study fears, desires, memories, emotions. But what about the *external* context in which we find ourselves? Especially in a performance situation – a job, an audition, an examination, or a sporting event – the environment outside the contestants' heads also affects why they succeed or fail. An embodied cognition approach would study how even seemingly insignificant aspects of an audition environment – such as the heat of the stage lights, the colour of the curtains and any bright brand-name logos – might influence performance.

Embodied cognition theory proposes that the mind cannot work separately from the physical world; that the senses provide the bridge to both our unconscious and our conscious thought processes. We psychologists and neuroscientists working in this field seek to show the influence that physical sensations have over our mental states and behaviour.[3] The mind-body connection is evident in everything we do.

Read the following passage:

> *The warmth of his handshake hid the heavy weight of his memories, but he had shot her down in cold blood and would never again sleep with a clean conscience.*

This sentence will not win any literary prizes with its awkward mix of metaphors, but let's look at it closely. The phrases *warmth of his handshake, heavy weight of his memories, in cold blood* and *clean conscience* show that our everyday speech is rooted in the connection between our physical experience and our psychological state.[4] It's difficult even to think of an emotion that doesn't carry with it a physical metaphor: isolation is cold, guilt is heavy, cruelty is hard.

Sensation shows that these relations between physical sensations and emotions and behaviours are real, not just metaphorical. Physical sensations such as warmth, distance, weight and many other subtle sensory experiences can (and do) activate and influence our judgements, emotional experiences and performances. This relationship between physical sensations and psychological experiences, though complex, reveals itself in a very particular way – as in the cold feeling that arises from loneliness.

A Cold, Lonely Night

Changes in temperature are known to affect our moods and behaviour. Pleasant, warm weather improves mood,[5] and heat is associated with aggression and crime rates.[6] In Shakespeare's *Romeo and Juliet*, Benvolio warns Mercutio of the air of sweltering violence in Verona's streets. 'I pray thee, good Mercutio, let's retire,' he says. 'The day is hot, the Capulets abroad, and, if we meet, we shall not 'scape a brawl, for now, these hot days, is the mad blood stirring.' The reality of the relationship is, as always, more complex, but the link itself is clear. Some classical psychologists still hold out against this finding, just as hard-liners hold out against the proof of global climate change, but environmental factors affect our mental states and thoughts in profound ways. As it turns out, small talk about the weather may not be so small after all. 'How about this weather?' is actually polite code for 'What's going on with you?' The answer to this seemingly innocent question may sometimes influence your judgements and decisions.

My mother used to love to tell this joke: A man and a woman had been dating for fifteen years. One day the woman asked the man, 'Don't you think it's time we got married?' The man answered, 'Absolutely, but who would marry us? It's a cold world out there.' Of course the woman meant that the two of them should marry, but, as the man points out, it's hard to find someone to be with. People sometimes use this expression, *It's a cold world out there*, when they're worrying about making bold changes in their lives, such as leaving a spouse or a job. What awaits them might be difficult, scary, or lonely – cold.

A friend once told me a sad little story from her youth. When she was thirteen, she was very excited about going to summer camp with her two best friends. But on the day they were supposed to leave, one of her friends fell ill and the other friend's family changed their plans; all of a sudden, she had to go to camp alone. Decades later, as we talked over hot tea in Tel Aviv, she recounted how cold she had felt every night that summer. Even though summers in Israel are very warm, her thin blanket wasn't enough to keep her comfortable. The connection between being lonely and feeling cold exists in many languages, in songs and poetry. Would my friend have experienced the temperature that summer differently if her friends had been there?

In North America, in Toronto, average daytime winter temperatures hover just below freezing. Residents contend with months of snow, ice, slush and serious windchill. This is the appropriate environment in which two researchers from the University of Toronto investigated the connection between being cold and feeling lonely. In two experiments, they examined whether physical temperature affects our psychological states, and also whether our feelings affect our perception of temperature.[7]

In the first experiment, the researchers asked 32 students to recall a situation in which they felt they were socially excluded and lonely. Think of not being invited to a party, not being asked to play a game with others, et cetera. Another 32 students were asked to think of a situation in which they were socially included, like being accepted into a club. The researchers then intentionally diverted the students' attention by telling them that the university maintenance staff wanted to know how hot or cold the room was. Would the students please estimate the temperature in the room? The students who recalled being socially excluded actually judged the room as colder than those who had recalled being socially included. The average estimate of those who remembered being excluded was 21.4°C, compared with an average estimate of 24.0°C by those who remembered being included. Yet they all had sat in exactly the same room.

So you see, emotional memories can influence your physical experience in the present. There is a powerful connection – even across time – between coldness and loneliness.

The researchers then wanted to go beyond summoning a memory of loneliness and recreate the experience in the present. So they used a brilliant way of making people feel left out. They invited one group of subjects to play a virtual ball-tossing game. Participants were asked to sit at the computer and play online with three other players at different locations. What they didn't know was that actually there were no other players; there was only a 'cruel' computer program designed to throw the digital 'ball' almost exclusively to the fictitious players in order to make the real person feel left out. The second group of participants got to play the same ball-tossing game, but with a computer program that was much less discriminatory in its ball tossing. These actual players received the ball intermittently throughout the game and, not surprisingly, had a much better time.

After the ball-tossing game, both groups were asked to participate in an ostensibly unrelated marketing task, to rate on a scale of 1 to 7 how much they desired five different products: hot coffee, hot soup, an apple, crackers and an icy Coke. Of course, the participants didn't know that the researchers were in fact interested in the effect of the earlier exclusion, and the researchers found that the 'excluded' students were significantly more likely to choose something hot than were the students who were not excluded. They concluded that warmth can be a remedy for loneliness.

Another group of researchers went to a deeper, more somatic level of studying exclusion and examined whether our skin temperature is actually lower when we feel left out.[8] They used the same virtual ball-tossing game as in the previous study, and again the computer was programmed for two conditions: inclusion and exclusion. In the inclusion game, participants received the ball every few throws, whereas in the exclusion game they never received the ball. Researchers measured participants' finger temperature during the experiment and found that participants who were excluded really became colder, and their finger temperatures decreased.

Going even further, the researchers conducted an experiment to answer the question, can holding something warm actually improve the feelings of people who have been excluded? They asked participants to play the same ball-tossing game and again divided them into excluded and included groups. This time, however, the researchers programmed the computer to stop after three minutes and display an alleged 'error'. When this happened, a researcher arrived at the participants' station holding a glass containing either cold or warm tea. All the participants requested his assistance, and the researcher then asked each participant to hold the beverage while he fixed the computer. Afterward, participants were asked to choose whether they had felt 'bad', 'tense', 'sad', or 'stressed' and to rate their feeling from 1 to 5. I would certainly have predicted that those who had been excluded would report more negative feelings than those who had been included, which was true for these participants. The amazing part of the results is that only those who were excluded and held a cold glass of tea had more negative feelings. For those who were excluded but had held a warm glass, their warm hands had warmed their feelings and, apparently, caused them to feel better.

Taken together, these results clearly show that feeling cold or warm is determined not only by the temperature of the room but also by your mental state. If you feel lonely, whether you are actually excluded from an activity or you are in the same room with individuals who do not share your opinions, choices and views, both your physical experience and your psychological experience actually change. Even if you just stand or sit far from someone or from a group, you feel isolated. The room becomes cold for you. In contrast, if you feel socially accepted, if you are in a room with people who share your opinions and preferences and views, or if you just sit close to someone, you feel that the room is warmer.

These findings have direct implications for how we live and should be especially important to teachers, educators and parents, who try to help children adjust to many situations. For example, children and adolescents sometimes feel lonely or isolated at school, and this feeling can lead to adjustment problems. Now that you know that warm temperatures can positively affect interpersonal interactions, you can help children not to feel as if they have been left out in the cold, and also help others feel warmer towards them. A simple action such as turning up the heat, asking children to put on sweaters, or having children share hot chocolate or hot lunches together can help support a positive interpersonal climate.

A young man I know told me that when he was a teenager his parents sent him to a psychologist to try to improve their relationship with him, but he was so uncomfortable in the doctor's office that he didn't even take off his coat for the first four months. It took him that long to warm up even to the psychologist. I myself have gone to a number of parties where I did not know anybody and felt quite lonely when entering the room. Many other people must have felt that way, too, as they didn't take off their coats either. Whether you're hosting a meeting or a party, make sure that the room is warm, at least at the beginning of a gathering. Serving warm drinks in a cold season and warm soup as a starter to a dinner might help. Lonely people – or people who are in new, unfamiliar social situations – need psychological warmth as well as physical warmth.

Temperature, Generosity and Trust:
Warm Your Hands and Open Your Heart

Could temperature affect more than just our opinions and feelings? Could it actually influence our behaviour? Could your daily ritual of drinking coffee change the likelihood that you would, say, spare some change for someone who asks for help outside your neighbourhood coffee shop? Does your warm morning tea help you start your day with a more open, positive attitude and even help you to trust others more? Williams and Bargh, the researchers at Yale who conducted the experiments with warm cups of coffee, devised a way to find out.[9]

They told participants that they were conducting a consumer marketing study and gave them a 'new product', a therapeutic pad. Participants were asked to hold the pad – which was either hot or cold – for a few moments, then evaluate its effectiveness and indicate whether they would recommend it to friends, family and strangers. But the most important part of the study was actually not the survey but the decision participants were asked to make after it. Individually, participants were given a choice between two rewards for participating in the study: a refreshment for themselves or a small gift certificate in the name of a friend they could choose.

The results were dramatic. Among those who held the cold pad, about 75 per cent chose a reward for themselves and only 25 per cent chose a gift for a friend. Of those who handled and reviewed the hot pad, 54 to 46 per cent chose a gift for a friend. That is a significant statistical difference in giving behaviour. Yet the only factor that was different in the experiment was the temperature of the pad in the participants' hands.

The results of this experiment reinforce the notion that philanthropy and charitable donations can be more emotional than rational. This is not to say that giving is purely an emotional urge, because of course it contains a large rational component. We are not prone to bouts of careless giving or fits of philanthropy, but we do give for many reasons: we may want to be liked and respected by the recipient; we may want to be perceived as generous in our communities; and we may want to feel important and needed. But this experiment, like most embodied cognition experiments, shows that there is a visceral influence on our actions, even those that we believe come from purely logical thought processes. It also shows that not only is there a significant emotional and subconscious component, but we can be compelled to act by mundane and subtle quotidian forces. In this case, the behaviour was triggered by the most trivial act (holding a therapeutic pad for a few moments).

Williams and Bargh led another investigation into whether holding a warm object would influence trust as well as generosity.[10] The bedrock of marriages, friendships and business relationships, trust can be hard-won and delicate, determined by many factors. Why do we build certain trusting relationships and not others? The decision to trust someone can be instantaneous and it can feel intuitive, but a little bit of warmth may help forge this important bond.

Researchers asked participants to hold a therapeutic pack that was either cold (15°C) or hot (41°C) in another supposed consumer product study. Then they had participants play a game in which some acted as investors and others as trustees. The investor decided how much money he or she would send to the trustee, who sat anonymously in the other room. The amount that the investor sent to the trustee was immediately tripled on receipt. Then the trustee had to decide how much money he or she returned. In each round of the game, the investors could invest any amount of money from none to one dollar in ten-cent increments. The more the investor invested, the greater the possibility he or she would get back more money, but only if the trustee chose to return it. Although participants believed they were participating in an investing game, they were really engaging in a test of trust. The more an investor trusted the trustee, the more money he or she would invest.

The results of the study were amazing. Those who touched the cold pack just before the game invested less money compared with those who touched the warm pack. The group with the cold pack did not so easily trust the trustees and were not so sure the trustees would return the investment. Holding a hot therapeutic pack, however, prompted people to feel more intimacy and trust others more readily.

The generosity, trust and intimacy effect of warmth seems to be short-term. Our minds are affected for only a little while by what our bodies feel, but, as I said earlier, what is brief is not necessarily unimportant. A snap judgement can have lasting consequences. The first step towards being able to control and work with these 'peas and cues' from our environment – and from other people – is to become aware of them.

Consider that you might be able to improve a first date – or an initial business meeting – by merely giving your companion a warm drink. You might also consider meeting at a Japanese restaurant that offers warm towels before you eat. Whenever you want another person to perceive you as warm or sympathetic, offer him a cup of warm tea or coffee. In negotiations over things such as salary, sales, or divorce, if you want the other side to compromise or show some generosity, you might offer a nice cup of tea or an espresso, rather than a cold soft drink. Doing so just may tip the scales in your favour.

Smooth Operators and Rough Customers: Texture

The Book of Genesis tells the story of Esau and Jacob, sons of the patriarch Isaac. As the elder son, Esau, a rough-mannered hunter, was entitled to the birthright or inheritance. Famished after a hunt, however, he sold his right to the blessing to Jacob, who was their mother's favourite, in exchange for a bowl of stew. When the time came for their aged, blind father to bestow the blessing on Esau, Jacob took his brother's place and, to deceive his father, wore a goatskin on his arms and neck in order to make them appear hairy like Esau's. Isaac could rely only on his sense of touch to read the situation, and remarked, 'The voice is the voice of Jacob, but the hands are the hands of Esau', and gave his blessing to Jacob.

This story demonstrates that not only is tactile perception essential for sensing the physical world but it can help us discern what goes on beneath the surface. Like Isaac, when it comes to figuring out many situations, we all are feeling our way around. The story also warns against depending too much on limited and contradictory sensory input in making an important judgement. It reminds us to question what our senses tell us when we're getting mixed messages, not to rely on assumptions or faith alone but to use our heads. And of course it also cautions us about putting more importance on an immediate, fleeting gratification, like a meal, than on the future satisfaction we would derive from a greater purpose or accomplishment, as Esau did when he allowed his stomach's physical desire to usurp his inheritance. 'Oh, what a tangled web we weave, when first we practise to deceive,' wrote Walter Scott. Beware of entangling yourself in complicated sit-uations. By relying on what your senses tell you, you may actually be deceiving yourself.

Our senses provide important information, vital to our survival, but we need to be conscious of the mixed messages they can convey and evaluate them with discernment.

Stories as well as metaphors alert us to the traps our senses can lay for us. Jacob was able to use embodied cognition to his advan-tage; Isaac surrendered his reason to his senses for a brief but crucial moment and changed the course of biblical history. Discerning the truth of a situation and of another person's motives (whether that person is aware of them or not) can be a challenge. The 'truth' is what we think we perceive through our senses and run through our minds, both consciously and unconsciously. Our verbal expressions represent our thoughts. *Rough day, soft-hearted, smooth sailing, a hard time, a soft landing, a hard bargainer, rough manners* – all these meta-phors involve tactile sensations and perceptions. But are these just random flourishes in our language, or does their existence connect to something deep in our nature?

The answer, it turns out, is skin-deep – and deeper. The human body's largest, most sensitive organ is the skin. It covers us entirely, from the delicate fingertips of a jazz pianist to the hardened soles of a fire walker. We want to 'stay in touch' with our loved ones, which usually means to stay in communication rather than in literal physical touch. The Gospel of Mark says that for Jesus to touch a person spiritually, that person must be willing to reach out and touch Jesus. Why is it not enough simply to see and hear Jesus to be affected by him? Of course generations who have come after Jesus lived have been touched through his words, but to the first followers the embodiment of his spirit in his person and the ability to touch and be touched by the spirit made flesh were compelling. To this day, we use touch-related words so often in language because touch is the most intimate way to experience and connect with the world.

Scientists have theorised that we used non-verbal communication, including touch, long before we used language. We begin progressing from non-verbal to verbal communication as soon as we are born. Through the touch of their parents and caregivers – hugs and kisses, nursing and holding – infants learn about the world around them. Psychologists have demonstrated the importance of touch in child development. Touch enhances feelings of security in children and improves their social skills. In famous, tragic cases of children who grew up in orphanages in Romania with hardly any human contact, the lack of touch stunted their emotional, social and cognitive development.[1]

Touch also influences adults' behaviour, such as compliance, altruism and risk taking. In one study salespeople in a supermarket approached shoppers and asked them to taste a new snack. While making the request they touched some of the shoppers lightly on the upper arm. That touch increased shoppers' willingness to try a sample and even to buy the snack.[2] A recent study found that a light tap on the shoulder increased financial risk taking in people, probably due to a resulting sense of enhanced security.[3] Another study found that waitresses who touched customers on the hand or on the shoulder for about a second received greater tips.[4] Yet the same brief touch did not influence customers' ratings of the waitresses or their ratings of the atmosphere of the restaurant; this suggests that the customers were not aware of the effect of the touch on their behaviour.

Touching another human being increases trust and cooperation. It reduces our perception of threat, increases our sense of security and relaxes us. Anxious people benefit from touching someone or holding hands. When people go to the doctor to have a potentially painful procedure, a light touch on the head or shoulders by a health-care provider can reduce their anxiety. A massage after a hard day at work helps me relax, even if my muscles are not particularly tense and I am not especially anxious.

The need to be touched has led scientists to try to design and create products that mimic the feeling of human touch. The 'hug shirt', for instance, communicates the sensation of touch for people who are physically separated: it is made of soft, pleasant-feeling materials and has sophisticated pressure sensors that are activated by various technologies such as mobile phone applications.[5] It even stimulates the emotional reactions that follow a hug, such as a decreased heart rate. Another invention uses a doll that transmits a hugging sensation to a child wearing a special 'cyberpyjama'.[6] People are willing to spend time and money to 'stay in touch' with techno-logical innovations as well as with the old-fashioned long embrace after being apart.

Our tactile sensations are not limited to human touch. We experience tactile sensations all the time, often without even noticing them. We sense softness, hardness, roughness and smoothness from wearing clothes and holding books, bags, computers, smartphones and iPads. We sense that cushions, pillows and chairs are hard or soft at home, in the office and in restaurants. We lie down at the end of the day on a bed whose softness or hardness we've chosen. We dry ourselves with our fluffy or rough towels, and at Pilates and yoga classes we exercise on thin or cushiony mats.

We also use tactile descriptions metaphorically. For example, *rough* describes a difficult, unpleasant situation or stretch of time, as the corresponding physical touch of a rough object can be uneven or harsh. We use the word *soft* when we describe someone who is easy to get along with or who can be easily moulded, like a soft, yielding substance. In contrast, *hard* is used to describe a rigid, difficult person who, like an unyielding material, cannot readily be changed.

Metaphors represent a deeper connection between our physical sensations and our behaviours and judgements. Several researchers examined whether metaphors such as *hard* and *soft* negotiations are not just a matter of speech and whether the texture of the objects we might touch influences our behaviour. Can a hard or soft chair influence how rigidly or flexibly we behave? Should we be careful where we sit when we have a difficult negotiation? We'll explore these questions throughout this chapter.

Hard People with Soft Spots

On every vacation, I go to San Diego to visit my daughter and grand-daughters. I love spending time with them, listening to their stories and telling them my own. During the day, when the children are at school, I love to be outside in the fresh air, and I make a habit of walking along the beach. San Diego's weather is beautiful, and you can walk for many miles on those gorgeous beaches. Usually, I walk with a good friend for about an hour and a half and then sit in one of the cafés along the beach.

There are two ways to walk along the beach: on the sand or on the boardwalk. The two routes are next to each other, but only the boardwalk is hard: it is made of wooden boards. My friend and I have no real preference, so sometimes we walk on the sand and sometimes we walk on the boardwalk.

I have noticed for quite some time that my friend can be very rigid on certain days, whereas on other days she can be much more flexible. Sometimes she does not mind what café we sit in, whereas at other times she insists that we stick to our original plan exactly. I always thought this was because she is moody, and I believed that she had bad days and good days. Recently, however, I noticed that she is more rigid on the days when we walk on the boardwalk than on those when we walk on the sand. Is it possible that the soft or hard tactile sensation on our feet softens or hardens my friend's behaviour?

A group of researchers from Harvard, Yale and MIT investigated this very question by conducting several experiments.[7] In the first experiment they devised a creative way to make their participants touch a soft or a hard object. They asked passers-by to watch and participate in a magic show. You probably remember that before a magician performs certain tricks, such as turning a handkerchief into doves or making money come out of a box, he often asks a member of the audience to touch the object to ascertain that there is nothing funny going on. So the researchers asked the passers-by to examine the object the magician was going to use. Half of the participants were asked to examine a hard block of wood and the other half a soft blanket. Then researchers told the participants that the magic show had been postponed and gave them another ostensibly unrelated task.

They were asked to read a passage describing an ambiguous inter-action between an employee and a boss. The participants were asked to rate several traits of the employee, some of which were related to rigidity and strictness. Those who had touched the soft blanket judged the employee to be less rigid and less strict (in other words, softer) than those who had touched the hard block. Yet all participants had been given the same scene to read. Participants from both groups rated all the other traits, such as outgoingness and seriousness, the same; they differed only on the traits related to strictness and rigidity.

The researchers wanted to find out whether the tactile sensation of hardness or softness would influence not only perception and judgement but also real behaviour – the kind exhibited during a negotiation or bargaining session. A soft bargainer sees the other negotiators as friends and seeks agreement even if it's necessary to compromise. That person will more easily modify his or her initial position in order to reach an agreement. In contrast, a hard bargainer sees the other negotiators as opponents. He or she usually does not trust them and does not want to change his or her initial position by making compromises.

The researchers examined how tactile sensations related to softness and hardness can influence how soft or hard we are in our bargaining. In this study the researchers did not ask the participants to hold a soft or a hard object but asked them to sit on either a wooden chair or a soft chair and to imagine they were at a car dealership, wanting to buy a certain car. Participants were asked to make two offers, assuming that the first offer was not accepted. Those who sat on a soft chair changed their initial offer more than did those who had sat on a hard chair. The soft seats made softer negotiators.

Softness and hardness are attributed not only to people and behaviours but also to some categories – gender identity, for example. Though gender roles have changed considerably, certain traits are still stereotypically attributed to men and women. One of these is softness. Much as we may dislike this prejudice, the fact is that women are perceived as being softer than men, and men as tougher than women.

A group of researchers conducted two studies to investigate whether our minds correlate a soft or hard physical sensation with female or male characteristics.[8] In the first study, participants were presented with eight sexually ambiguous faces on a computer screen and asked to indicate whether they were male or female. They were also asked to squeeze a ball during the task, because the experiment was supposedly examining the influence of performing a task on face perception. Participants were divided into two groups, one of which was given a soft ball and the other a harder ball. Those who squeezed the hard ball were more likely to categorise the ambiguous faces as male. In other words, the tactile sensation of softness or hardness influenced whether the participants perceived a person as male or female.

In the second study, participants were asked again to categorise faces as male or female. This time the faces were presented not on the computer screen but on paper, on which the participants were to write their answers with a pen. Participants in one group were told to press the pen hard since there was carbon paper underneath and the researchers needed two copies. Those in the other group were asked to press gently and not damage the carbon paper underneath. Researchers found again that those who pressed the pen hard categorised faces as males more often than did those who pressed the pen gently.

So soft–hard tactile sensation influences categorisation of male and female identity. Might we find similar results regarding other categories that are stereotypically associated with soft and hard? Several researchers examined this question with two social categories: academic disciplines and political affiliation.

Academic disciplines are categorised as hard and soft. The natural and physical sciences are colloquially called 'hard sciences', whereas the social sciences are 'soft sciences'. I don't like this dichotomy, especially since psychology is often considered a social or soft science even though we psychologists run controlled experiments and measure quantitatively just as life or physical scientists do.

In the political arena, in the United States, Republicans generally have more hard-line views on the economy and foreign relations as well as on social issues such as abortion or same-sex marriage and are regarded as harder than Democrats, who are perceived by most Americans as softer and more compassionate and empathetic.[9]

In one study researchers examined whether tactile sensations of softness or hardness would influence participants' identification of people as Democrats or Republicans or as physicists (hard science) or historians (soft science).[10] In one experiment, they showed participants photos of four male and four female faces and asked them to guess each one's political affiliation while squeezing either a soft ball or a hard ball. The results were similar to the findings regarding the perceived gender of faces: those who squeezed a soft ball identified more faces as Democrats.

In the next experiment, participants were presented with photos of professors and asked to identify them as physicists or historians. Compared with those who squeezed a soft ball, participants who squeezed a hard ball classified more faces as those of physicists.

These findings suggest that soft or hard sensations do influence our categorisation process. The tactile sensations of softness and hardness activate the psychological concepts of soft and hard. These physical sensations influenced how people perceived an interaction as soft or hard, and how they categorised individuals. The sensations affected people's actual behaviour.

Take the Rough with the Smooth

One day my three-year-old granddaughter, Natalie, noticed that her father was in a bad mood. Now, moods are very complicated things (if they can even be called 'things'). There are researchers who spend their entire careers studying moods, but as a 'child psychologist', Natalie had an instant explanation for her daddy's doldrums – he was angry since he had hair on his face. She was referring to his stubble from not shaving, but I thought this was so adorable, in the way that children's ideas often are. Of course he would be upset, with his face feeling rough, Natalie thought.

In many languages, we associate roughness with difficulty, frustration and pain, and this association could indicate a deeper, embodied connection of sensation to word.

When I was a young soldier in the air force, my unit worked in shifts. The night shift was from 7.00 p.m. to 8.00 a.m. the next day, when we returned home and had a free day and night; then we went back to the barracks the next morning. The night shifts were convenient for me and my class schedule at the university, but even so, I hated them. At night, we were divided into two groups, and each group was given four hours of sleep in a small room. I distinctly remember the blankets and sheets on the beds as very rough. At a certain point we realised that we could bring our own towels, pillowcases and sheets, which made our sleep more comfortable and pleasant. I started thinking that the shifts were not so bad and enjoyed the time I spent on them with my friends much more. The atmosphere became smoother; we worked in harmony with far fewer arguments and conflicts. We all had realised that it was more pleasant to sleep on smooth rather than rough sheets and blankets, but we hadn't thought the change would improve our waking lives as well. Now, many years later, I believe that the tactile sensations of roughness and smoothness influenced our behaviour and interactions. We had slept not on the wrong *side* of the bed but on the wrong *sheets* on the bed.

A group of researchers investigated whether touching a smooth or rough object would influence participants' perceptions of a personal interaction as rough or smooth.[11] To prime the sensation of rough or smooth, the experimenters gave participants jigsaw puzzles to complete, telling them this was a cognitive test. Half of the participants received puzzles with glossy, smooth pieces, while the other half received pieces that were covered in coarse-grained sandpaper.

After working with the puzzles, they were asked to participate in another study, which was ostensibly different from the 'cognitive' test. Participants read a transcript of an interaction between two people that was deliberately ambiguous, somewhere between a friendly conversation and an argument. They then had to indicate whether the interaction was friendly or unfriendly, competitive or cooperative, a discussion or an argument.

The students who had handled the sandpaper puzzles judged the interaction to be more competitive, unfriendly and argumentative compared with the smooth-puzzlers, who found the interaction friendlier and non-competitive. Although all participants read the same transcript, merely touching a rough or a smooth object influenced their perceptions of the interaction as smooth or rough. There was no difference between the two groups in their evaluations of how familiar the people they'd read about were with one another. Only aspects relating to rough or smooth were skewed after the participants had been primed by the jigsaw puzzles.

Why Texture Matters: The Scaffolding of Experience

Without our awareness, the textures of the various objects we constantly touch influence our judgements, perceptions and behaviour. Touching rough, smooth, hard, or soft objects influences how rough or smooth, hard or soft we perceive a situation to be and how hard or soft our behaviour is. As incredible as these results sound, they are logical from the point of view of embodied cognition. They suggest that metaphors and abstract conceptualisations are related and grounded in our bodily experiences. That is, the physical sensations of texture are the building blocks of the abstract concepts with the same names. The concept of a rough relationship, for instance, is built on the experience of rough texture, which is learned very early in life.

A building, even the tallest one, starts with a foundation, and is built, layer by layer, floor upon floor upon floor, upon this foundation. Similarly, through the process of scaffolding, children develop meaning for these concepts in direct relation to their physical underpinnings. Children learn concepts through physical sensations. They learn that some tactile sensations are soft, like their mothers' touch and their teddy bears' fur. They learn that a doctor's examining table is hard and the experience there, perhaps receiving an injection, is rough. These sensations become the scaffold upon which the abstract concepts are built. It is almost as if they create a mental file under the same name – 'smoothness' – in which every emotional experience is included with its corresponding physical experience. When we become adults, tactile sensations all evoke emotions that are related to these early sensory experiences, and thus influence our behaviour, emotions and judgements. Our minds read the old file, and we act accordingly.

Abstract concepts may become grounded in our sensory-motor experiences when physical sensations activate specific areas in the brain. If physical sensations are in fact the building blocks of abstract knowledge and metaphorical expressions are born from sensory-motor inspiration, then the same brain regions that are activated during the tactile physical sensation (rough–smooth, hard–soft) will be activated when we use the corresponding metaphors (*rough relationships, hard day*). On the other hand, if abstract concepts are not grounded in our sensory experiences and metaphors are just random flourishes of speech, then different areas of the brain will be activated when we touch a rough object and when we use the metaphor *rough day*. Using functional magnetic resonance imaging (fMRI), researchers recently examined this exact question.[12]

The fMRI scanner measures the change in blood flow to neurons in different parts of the brain, which indicates that those areas are working on information they're receiving. This machine allows researchers to examine the activity of the brain during cognitive and emotional behaviours such as judgement, decision making, problem solving, memorising and reading various types of texts, among others.

In this recent study the researchers chose 54 sentences that contained tactile metaphors – such as 'She had a rough day' – and paired them with sentences with the same meaning but without the metaphors, such as 'She had a bad day'. Participants lay in the scanner while wearing headphones through which the various sentences were read to them. The researchers found that the brain regions that were activated when the participants heard sentences with texture metaphors were the same brain regions that are activated when people sense texture through touch.

These results provide evidence that the brain processes metaphors in the same areas that it 'feels' or notices specific sensory input. These areas are not activated when we process sentences that have the same meaning but don't use tactile metaphors.

To Shave or Not to Shave?

Life is a series of negotiations. These findings have real-world implications for business negotiations. Consider the types of chairs on which you and your opposition sit during an important negotiation. If the chair is soft, there is a better chance that the person who sits on it will be more flexible and more likely to change an initial attitude or offer. But if you're sitting in cold, hard chairs, you're likely to see each other as unfriendly and unyielding.

But the implications go beyond chairs, of course. Think of all the things we hold in our hands. We make contact with so many objects, and we do not even realise it. I always carry my handbag, and it is usually soft. I sometimes put it aside, but more often I keep it in one of my hands. In contrast, we often come to business meetings with our computers, holding these hard objects during the whole meeting. Might they be predisposing us to take hard lines in a discussion? Another hard object we often hold is our phone, though its case might be smooth, rough, or a little padded. Does a smooth case make us more relaxed when using our phones to talk with our family and friends?

We also have to negotiate daily with our children, spouses, co-workers and even friends. We have to determine how many hours kids will get to use the computer or watch TV, at what time they will go to bed, how much money they can spend, and their curfew after a party. We discuss with our spouses the family budget, vacation plans and how to raise the kids. At work, we evaluate projects, contracts, terms and conditions, hiring and firing; we negotiate with customers and fight for benefits.

When we negotiate, sometimes we are soft, even too soft, and on other occasions we are hard, even too hard. Have you ever decided not to budge on bedtime but later changed your position? Do you usually stand your ground, ignoring the other person's arguments? The embodied cognition studies suggest that our perceptions of a situation can be influenced by simple contact with rough or smooth, soft or hard objects in the environment. Our attitudes can change when we use smooth things, such as velvety towels, or rough ones, such as coarse sheets. It is not news that smoothly ironed linen sheets are pleasant to the touch, but this research suggests that the smoothness of the sheets might affect how you feel about your significant other who joins you in bed. To help smooth over any tensions from the day, you might even shave your face or legs or wear nightclothes made of soft, silky fabrics for that extra nudge of influence.

In domestic life, these results might help us with our children, who like soft toys. Psychologists call security objects, such as blankets or soft toys to which young children develop attachments, 'transitional objects'. These objects enhance children's feelings of security and reduce their anxiety, especially in unfamiliar or scary situations. Simply touching soft objects, not even necessarily transitional objects, might soften children's behaviour and perceptions of situations. Think about that the next time you buy your child or grandchild a toy.

Older children might also benefit from touching soft objects. Indeed, I often hear from school psychologists and teachers about their creative efforts to help children with attention deficit or behavioural problems. One of their methods is to let the children touch, squeeze and play with soft objects such as squishy balls during class, which, these professionals believe, improves the children's concentration and reduces aggression.

A psychologist friend of mine had a therapist, who she adored, who always held a cat during their sessions. In the beginning it bothered my friend a bit since she is not a cat person, but she got used to it and went to that therapist for years. She found the therapist to be an extremely accepting, non-judgemental and empathetic woman who always saw the good side, even when a situation was quite difficult. No doubt these qualities reflected her empathetic and soft personality, but did her behaviour have anything to do with the fact that she was petting the soft fur of her cat?

Animals are sometimes used in the therapeutic process to help patients improve their social and emotional skills.[13] There is no doubt that interacting with and taking care of live animals have positive influences on us. Studies have demonstrated that the simple act of petting and touching animals lowers heart rate and blood pressure, reduces stress and anxiety, and aids relaxation.[14] If you should consider adopting a pet, think not only of the additional responsibilities but also of the benefits pets will bring to the whole family. All you have to do is pet their soft coats to bring out their own soft nature – and yours.

3

Don't Take This Lightly: The Importance of Weight

I am a psychologist, not a weightlifter, but, believe it or not, the decision to write this book came to me while I was in the gym 'pumping iron'. Nothing crazy, just the basic resistance training I do several times a week in order to stay healthy and fit. Unlike professional weightlifters, who are extremely focused on their movements, I let my thoughts wander while performing my repetitions. Writing a book had been on my mind for a long time, but suddenly for some reason, on that particular day, in between leg curls, I knew I had to do it. I realised how important it was for me to present the amazing findings that have accumulated in recent years about how physical sensations affect our emotions and behaviour.

But why did I think about it then, rather than while I was lying in bed or walking down the street? Is it possible that any issue seems more important to us when we think about it while carrying a heavy object?

You could say I had been *weighing my options*. Language reflects metaphorical association of importance with physical weight. *Weighing our options* means we're considering what is best for us to do. We might ask someone else to *weigh in*, if his or her opinion *carries a lot of weight* for us. Weight is serious. We describe decisions as *heavy* when they have important consequences. We say that someone important *throws his weight around*. We say that negativity *weighs us down*, and we call our problems *burdens*. We feel *encumbered* when others are relying on us, and we feel relief when someone helps us and takes the *weight off our shoulders*. A classic example is the ancient image of Atlas the Titan, his every sinew and tendon straining to hold up the Earth on his back, the fate of humanity dependent on him carrying the *weight of the world*.

These metaphors are not just figures of speech. Their abstract concepts are grounded in our physical sensations, and our concept of importance specifically is anchored to our physical experience of feeling weight.

Several groups of researchers investigating embodiment crafted experiments that examined the association between physical weight and importance.[1] In one experiment, the participants were asked to evaluate a job candidate based on a CV. All participants received the same CV, but half of them received it on a clipboard that weighed only 340g, while the other half, the 'heavy group', got the CV on a 2kg clipboard. Those who received the heavy clipboard rated the candidate as better qualified, with a more serious interest in the position.

There was no difference between the two groups when they were asked whether the candidate was sociable and would get along with his co-workers. The physical weight affected only the participants' judgement of traits related to performance and seriousness. The heavier clipboard had a powerful influence, but it was limited to perceptions of seriousness and qualifications.

For the second experiment, the researchers ventured outside the university. They asked passers-by on the street to complete a survey about funding for various public issues and to indicate whether each cause should receive more or less funding than the others. The survey included issues of general importance, such as education and air pollution, alongside more specialised issues, such as postal workers' salaries and the hardly pressing question of the regulation of public bathroom sinks. As before, half of the participants filled out this survey on a light clipboard, weighing 450g, and the other half on a heavy clipboard, weighing 1.6kg.

The heavy clipboard was influential again, but this time only men were affected by which clipboard they held, and only when judging the general issues. Women wanted to fund the social issues no matter how heavy or light the clipboard they held. Men, on the other hand, felt that the general issues were of greater importance when they were holding the heavier board. For them, the physical weight of the clipboard influenced the metaphorical weight they gave to the various issues. Studies have shown that women are more supportive of funding social welfare, health and education and of policies for disadvantaged groups.[2] They believed that social issues should be funded, and therefore the weight of the clipboard did not influence their decision. In contrast, men, who are relatively less concerned with social issues, were influenced by the heavier clipboard.

A group of Dutch researchers asked a large group of students to fill out questionnaires that estimated the value of various foreign currencies.[3] Here, too, half of the participants filled out their questionnaires on light clipboards, 660g, while the other half used clipboards weighing 1kg. The students who held the heavier clipboards valued the various currencies significantly higher than the students who held the lighter clipboards. Weight in their hands added 'weight' to the currencies.

In a second experiment, these researchers asked students to read a scenario about a university committee that made decisions regarding grants to students who travel abroad; the committee did not let students express their opinions about the decisions. Participants were asked how important it was to them that the students be allowed to express their opinions before the committee. All participants answered standing up, holding the questionnaire on a clipboard; half of them were given a heavy clipboard and the other half a lighter one. Compared with those who held a light clipboard, participants who held a heavy clipboard said it was more important for the committee to consider the students' input. Again, the weight of the clipboard influenced their judgements.

As a dean of students and a member of the executive board of my university, I dealt with the grants given to students and with students' requests to participate in university decisions, especially the decisions that directly affected them. After all, the size of a grant and the way it is distributed directly affect a student's life and academic career. Based on my experience with students, I would have thought that most of them would say that any committee needs to listen to the students it serves, regardless of the weight of the clipboard they were holding. However, these results together with the results of the other studies clearly suggest that without our awareness, we associate importance with heavy weight.

These studies also demonstrate that the association between importance and physical weight is not only semantic but an actual part of our connected, scaffolded experience of the world. The sensation of physical weight, by triggering interconnected mental and emotional associations, influences our opinions about value, importance and seriousness.

Don't Judge a Book by Its Cover (Judge It by Its Weight!)

So heavy things influence our importance judgements. To put it like a scientist, the sensation of heavy weight activates the abstract concept of importance, and consequently leads to attribution of importance. Does this association flow both ways? Does the abstract concept of importance influence our perception of an object's weight? A group of Dutch researchers investigated this very question.[4] They conducted their research in two parts. In the first study they asked participants to hold a book in their hands and estimate its weight. All participants were told that this book was used by the faculty, but half of the students were told that it was an *important* book, whereas the other half were not told anything about its importance. Compared with those who heard nothing about importance, the students who were told that the book was important estimated it as heavier.

The researchers then wanted to explore whether this association between importance and weight would be found if the participants only looked at the book. So they ran the experiment a second time and created a control group that simply looked at the book. They found that only students who were holding the book were influenced by being told it was 'important'. The weight-importance connection wasn't activated unless the participants were holding the book in their hands. These results demonstrate that the abstract concept of importance is embodied in the physical sensation of weight.

Taken with the previous studies, these findings show that the association between importance and weight is bidirectional. Physical weight activates importance, and the concept of importance activates the physical sensation of weight. These findings can shed light on some of our behaviours. Do backpackers who travel the world with their possessions on their backs consider their experiences more significant because they are carrying a heavy weight? Would they feel the same if they were travelling light? If you carry a lot of paperwork home with you every day in a heavy briefcase, are you more likely to feel burdened at home, unavailable to your family?

These findings have other implications too. Let's start with CVs

– this research shows that stationery matters. Of course, the content of a CV has a significant weight (metaphorically, of course), and if a person is not qualified for a job, the actual physical weight of the CV probably won't help. But in many cases there are a lot of qualified candidates for a job, and the interviewer must choose a few CVs that seem the most promising, since it is usually impossible to interview all the qualified applicants. Now that you know that the heavier something is, the more important it seems subconsciously, using heavier-weight stationery seems like a good thing to do to influence a potential employer. Sometimes all you need is the slightest edge to get over the top – and creative use of the influence of weight could do that for you.

These findings might bother you, of course, because we would really like to believe that job candidates are judged on their merit alone. Unfortunately, however, we know that this is often not the case, and that factors like gender, sexual orientation, age and race, for example, can bias our decisions, including those about hiring. Could the weight of the paper you use for your CV really cost you a job or make you more likely to be hired? The psychological concept of bias can refer to anything that influences a person's judgement in a certain direction, however subtle and unconscious that influence might be. Today many CVs are sent by e-mail, and for documents read on a computer screen, physical weight is not an issue. This may help to equalise the field, but perhaps sending in your CV physically – printed on good-quality paper – to support your online application would still make a difference in how you are perceived. After all, the physical presence of your CV could give you more weight in the mind of the evaluator.

As a psychology professor who has been grading papers for almost 30 years, I have asked myself after learning of these findings if I could have been influenced by the weight of the paper students used.

I'm in the habit of reading while sitting down and holding the paper in my hands rather than setting it on the desk. Psychology is not mathematics, and the grade is ultimately my subjective evaluation of the ideas presented in the paper and the way the work is written. If, without my noticing, I was psychologically influenced by the physical weight of the papers, that would be ironic. Who knows – perhaps I gave a grade of A– to a student who might otherwise have merited a B+ because the assignment was handed in on heavier, smoother paper.

In spite of the predominance of e-mail, there are still many documents that are read as hard copies. The next time you are submitting a CV, a paper, a proposal, or the like for evaluation, or sending a letter, consider giving the content some extra weight by using thick paper or presenting it in a heavy folder. You may distinguish it favourably from competitors' entries.

Although these days many petitions and surveys are conducted online, we are still approached fairly often on the street by people with clipboards and pencils who ask us to stop for just a minute to answer some questions or to sign a petition. Petitions deal with a range of issues, political, social, educational and environmental, some more important to us than others, and some that are not important to us at all. Many people simply do not stop when approached by volunteers with clipboards. Those who do stop, however, may well decide whether to sign a petition or not, especially on an issue about which they do not have strong feelings, based on nothing more than the weight of the clipboard.

We often carry weight, probably more than we realise: packages from the grocery store, heavy bags and our children in our arms. Next time you reach a decision when you are carrying something relatively heavy, ask yourself whether you would have made a similar decision if you had been unencumbered.

I carry a handbag that contains my computer, phone, wallet and makeup, and a hairbrush and several papers I want to read and a book; and who knows what else. It is really heavy. When I step into my office, I set it aside, but while walking to the classroom and back to the office, I generally carry it with me. At the end of my lectures, students often approach me to bounce ideas off me or make special requests. I usually ask them to walk with me to my office and talk along the way. I wonder whether their ideas and requests seem more important to me when I carry the heavy bag than they would when I am sitting in my office, unencumbered.

Studies on this topic have the potential to change how we look at our relationship to our environment. What we value as important has a holy place in our minds. We organise our entire lives around activities we think are important, and therefore it is harder to accept that we are illogical in our approach to them. While a heavy clipboard may not radically change our beliefs, it is unsettling to learn that they can be influenced at all! We need to become more aware of these subtle mental machinations so that our decisions can be more our own, and not influenced by simple factors such as weight.

Confessions of a Heavy Heart: Physical Weight and Secrets

I felt much better after I talked to him and got a load off my mind.
I felt I had to unburden myself and reveal my secret.
I was weighed down by keeping his secret.

United States Air Force First Lieutenant Josh Seefried had a secret. His friends in the air force didn't know he was gay, and they didn't know how isolated and ashamed of hiding his sexual orientation Josh felt when he was occasionally asked if he had a girlfriend at home. Lieutenant Seefried kept his sexuality a secret for many years due to a

US military policy then in effect known as 'Don't ask, don't tell', which banned openly gay men and women from serving in the military from 1993 to 2011. He had kept this secret from his friends and colleagues because he knew that openly declaring his homosexuality would lead to his dishonourable discharge, and maybe even prosecution.

In order to keep his secret, Lieutenant Seefried sought support from fellow gay and lesbian recruits via popular social networks under the pseudonym J.D. Smith. Realising that many active-duty service members kept their sexual orientations hidden, Josh founded a support network called OutServe. There he promoted equality and the repeal of 'Don't ask, don't tell'. J.D. was known in the popular news media, even appearing for interviews with his face obscured, but his true identity remained a secret for two years. On 18 December 2010, after the US Congress decided to repeal the policy, Josh revealed that he was J.D. Smith. He told a CNN reporter that he could now go back to work 'with that burden lifted off my shoulders and not have to worry about it anymore.'

New research indicates that Lieutenant Seefried's reference to his secret as a burden is more than a coincidental metaphor. Throughout our lives we keep personal and professional secrets. We all have secrets that are small and insignificant or enormously consequential. There are family secrets; painful, traumatic secrets, such as being abused or molested as a child; and illnesses that are kept secret. I've heard stories of breadwinners who get fired and keep it a secret from their spouses and children, pretending to go to work each morning.

People keep secrets mainly because the consequences of revealing the secrets can be damaging to themselves or others. Some feel ashamed and keep a secret for fear of being ridiculed or discriminated against. Others might keep a secret because they do not want to be seen to deviate from social norms or hurt others.

Keeping a secret, whether it is your secret or someone else's, is a mental burden, a load on your mind. It requires that you always be on guard, so that the secret doesn't slip out. Yet people often fail to keep secrets and sometimes decide to reveal their own. General wisdom holds that confessions are good for us; people feel better after they confess. Indeed, psychologists have found that carrying secrets for a long time is detrimental to one's physical well-being. There are, however, many cases in which secrets must be kept or the people involved will be seriously hurt.

People frequently report feeling as though a weight has been lifted off their chests after revealing a secret. Latin singer Ricky Martin posted a public statement on his official website in 2010 revealing that he was a 'fortunate homosexual man'. He explained that he used to hide his sexual orientation as a result of pressure society imposed on him and wrote, 'I was carrying within me for a long time things that were too heavy for me to keep inside.'

So if our emotions are grounded in our physical sensations, is it possible that we experience secrets not only as emotional burdens but as physical ones as well? A group of researchers posited that those who keep important secrets will display behaviours that are similar to those of people who actually carry a physical weight.[5]

Other experiments had demonstrated that people who carried heavy backpacks estimated a hill as steeper and a distance as greater than those who did not carry a weight.[6] This makes perfect sense. Climbing a hill with a heavy backpack requires more physical effort, so naturally the hill seems steeper. It is usually very easy to travel from one room to another, but with a heavy parcel it can be quite difficult, and we may find ourselves counting every step. We then estimate the distance as farther than it really is or than we would otherwise perceive it to be. In order to examine whether keeping secrets has an influence similar to that of carrying a heavy weight, the researchers conducted four studies.

In the first study, researchers asked participants to recall a secret. Half were asked to recall a meaningful and important personal secret and the other half a small personal secret. Participants were then asked to estimate the steepness of a hill in an ostensibly unrelated study. The results clearly demonstrated that those who thought about meaningful and important secrets estimated the hill as steeper. The important secrets were indeed perceived as physical weight and consequently influenced the people as an actual physical weight would have: the hills seemed steeper to those carrying a secret.

In a second experiment, the researchers asked half of the participants to recall an important, meaningful secret and the other half a trivial secret. They then asked them to toss a beanbag into a container placed about nine feet away from them in order to examine their perception of distance. The idea behind this task was that if people perceived the distance as farther, they would overshoot. If they perceived the distance as closer, they would not toss the beanbag far enough. The researchers found that, like those who carry an actual weight, those who recalled an important secret perceived the distance as farther and therefore overshot the beanbag.

In the third study, researchers focused on one particular secret, infidelity. They recruited participants who had recently reported being unfaithful and asked them to what extent they were troubled by their infidelity and how much they thought about it. Researchers then asked participants to estimate how much effort and energy they would need to perform six common tasks. Half of the tasks required physical effort, such as climbing the stairs with groceries or helping someone move, and half required no physical effort, such as giving someone directions or change.

The more participants said they thought about their infidelity and were bothered by it, the more effort and energy they estimated they would need to perform physical tasks. This difference was not found for tasks that did not require physical effort. In other words, the more people felt that the secret bothered them and was a burden, the more difficult they thought quotidian physical tasks would be. One could argue that people who are occupied with their secrets are not in a generous state of mind – not open to helping others – but these studies demonstrate that this was not the case. People who were keeping a secret were still willing to help others when the help did not demand physical effort.

In their fourth experiment, the researchers asked 30 gay men to participate in a study dealing with self-presentation. They asked the participants to answer questions while they were being filmed. Half of the participants were asked to conceal their sexual orientation, while the other half were asked to conceal another trait, extroversion. The idea was that sexual orientation is a more important and meaningful secret than the fact that one is an extrovert. At the end of the experiment, participants were asked to help move books out of the laboratory under the pretence that the lab was being relocated. But really the researchers were measuring how many books each participant moved: the more books he moved, the more willing he was to make a physical effort. Those who concealed their sexual orientation moved fewer books than those who concealed their extroverted personalities. The more important, meaningful secret affected the participants like a physical weight.

The Final Weigh-In: Lighten Up!

People who carry secrets feel physically burdened and experience a sensation similar to constantly carrying a heavy weight on their shoulders. Big, consequential secrets, such as one's sexual orientation, a traumatic experience, infidelity and illness, weigh us down and feel like an actual physical burden.

In order to ease the burden, the keeper of a secret may find it helpful to write in a journal, speak with a therapist, or confide in a close, trusted friend. Online support groups or other safe outlets can provide very necessary release, unburdening us while allowing us to maintain anonymity. The weight of secrets can be very hard to carry; these studies teach us that it is important to release those burdens because they physically affect us.

Slow Down, Red Ahead:
Red and Performance

Who has not been moved by colours, by the changing blues of the sky, or the greens of the sea, or the hues of a lover's eyes? It is fascinating to try to unpack the human experience of colour. A physicist would tell you that colour has to do with the wavelength and frequency of the beams of light reflecting and scattering off a surface. An ophthalmologist would tell you that colour has to do with the anatomy of the perceiving eye and brain, that colour does not exist without a cornea for light to enter and colour-sensitive retinal cones for the light waves to stimulate. A neurologist might tell you that colour is the electrochemical result of nervous impulses processed in the occipital lobe in the rear of the brain and translated into optical information. As a psychologist, however, I will tell you that colour is a critical factor in your environment that stimulates and influences you in hundreds of ways every day.

We all know anecdotally that colour is important and that colour is symbolic. We often use colours in metaphors, just as we use temperature, weight and texture. An English phrase book is rich with colourful idioms such as *tickled pink, yellow-bellied, in the red, green with envy* and *grey areas*. A Crayola crayon box bursts with creative names of colours such as Cadet Blue, Radical Red, Royal Purple, Shocking Pink, Screamin' Green and Unmellow Yellow. Our environment, with its colourful uniforms, flags, logos and signs, affects the way we process certain feelings and emotions.

The classic film *The Wizard of Oz* begins in black and white, but after the tornado picks up Dorothy's house and transports it to another land, she opens the door and steps into a new world of colour. In real life, too, we often see things anew after going through a dramatic challenge or crisis. The complexion – and complexity – of the world around us is always changing. Colour is tied to identity. Republicans and Democrats claim red states and blue states. Where the Crips and Bloods gangs rule in some neighbourhoods in Los Angeles, wearing the 'wrong' colour can get you killed. The threat of Communism in the 1950s was known as the 'Red Scare', and, in contrast, Les Bleus, the nickname of the French national sports teams, provides a unifying hue for a diverse nation. Colour is the calling card of every sports team, from Celtic green to the purple and gold of the Los Angeles Lakers and the colours of the St Louis Blues and the Cincinnati Reds. Fans identify their heroes and each other by the colours they wear on their backs.

Some colours have different meanings in different cultures. The colour orange is sacred for Buddhists; it is the national colour of Holland; but for me, a daughter of citrus growers, it was simply the colour of the fruit. I associated orange with trips to the grove with my father or outings to the packing house, where I watched workers pack thousands of oranges into crates. This simple association of orange with fruit changed, however, for almost all Israelis in 2005 when the Disengagement Plan was enacted to evacuate all Israelis from the Gaza Strip. Many of the settlers in Gaza strongly opposed the plan and had to be forcibly evicted from their homes by the Israeli army. At that time, the colour the settlers adopted was orange. This colour signalled a very clear political view, and this association between the colour orange and the political view was so strong that other people who believed in the Disengagement Plan and disagreed with the settlers' resistance stopped wearing orange. One of my friends who loved the colour orange and had some orange shirts and trousers gave these items away following the Disengagement, saying she could not wear them anymore. In another political action, Burmese Buddhist monks adopted the colour orange for their peaceful protest against the military junta running their country's government, which became known as the Saffron Revolution. On the other side of the globe, Catholic separatists of Northern Ireland view orange as the colour of the Protestant oppressors, the Orangemen.

Yet some colours, such as red, have near-universal associations. New experiments have revealed the surprising influence of colours in a wide range of behaviours. The studies I'll describe show not only that the symbolism of colour is deeply embedded in language but also that associations with colour are much more complex than they seem at first glance.

In the Red

Red is not just any colour. It is the colour of our deepest, most visceral emotions. In many cultures, it represents passion and danger, threat and lust. Red is so intense that we feel its power intuitively. You notice the reddest of red lipsticks even at the most crowded party. Even when speeding, you will usually spot a stop sign in time to screech to a halt.

Throughout history, we humans have associated red with aggression. We talk about *raising a red flag* to alert co-workers to trouble in a project and about *seeing red* when we refer to the psychological state of anger or irritation. And as scientists have discovered, the colour red affects our sexual behaviour, our physical performance, and even our performance on mathematical and verbal tests.

Red and IQ Tests

Our society is obsessed with tests that are meant to measure our abilities. The eleven-plus, SATs, GCSEs, A-levels. Tests are also sometimes given to job candidates. Although we adults might not remember the tests we took (or we would prefer to forget them), our children and grandchildren are constantly subjected to tests to measure vocabulary, spelling and the understanding of relationships between words, as well as tests to assess knowledge of algebra, geometry and calculus.

Besides our ability, skills and knowledge, however, other factors, such as colour, influence our performance on these tests. We are usually aware of the influence on our performance of factors like our own fatigue or disruptive noise. But consider an old riddle, which had to be spoken: 'What is black and white and red all over?' The old answer, from an age when news was printed in black and white on paper, was, of course, a newspaper: *red* being pronounced the same as *read*. But the new answer is a test that someone has done poorly on.

Many studies have shown that women's performance on mathematical tests is impaired when participants are reminded of their sex simply by being asked before taking the test to indicate it on a test booklet.[1] A similar phenomenon occurs when African Americans are asked to indicate their race at the beginning of a test: their performance on mathematical tests decreases.[2] These studies demonstrate that the simple act of reminding individuals that they belong to a certain group (females or African Americans) that has been stereotyped as 'not good at maths' is enough to decrease their performance on a test – even for students who have strong maths skills. Yet participants were absolutely unaware of the influence of the stereotype on their performance. This phenomenon is known as *stereotype threat*. Just as stereotype threat can negatively affect performance without our awareness, so can the colour red.

A team of American and German researchers headed by Andrew J. Elliot set out to explore this connection between the colour red and performance on achievement tests.[3] They conducted several experiments, some in the United States and some in Germany. In the first experiment, they invited 71 American undergraduates to participate and tested each participant individually. The experimenter told the students that they would be given an anagram test, in which they would be required to unscramble rearrangements of letters (like *belta*) into words (like *table*). The anagrams were neither particularly easy nor especially difficult. After a practice test, participants were randomly divided into three groups.

Although all the students received the same anagram test, there was one important difference among the groups: the colour of the participant number. The key was this: numbers were written at the top of each page. For one group of students, the number was written in red; for another group the number was written in green; for a third group it was written in black. Again, this was the only difference among the three groups. In order to make sure that the students noticed the numbers, they were asked to double-check the number on each page (because, the researcher said, the pages would be separated later). The students were then told to begin the test, which they were given five minutes to complete.

The results were incredible – the subtle red test number had a dramatic effect. Students whose tests had a red number at the top of each page performed significantly worse, solving fewer anagrams than those who had a green or a black participant number.* The experiment had been crafted to control all testing variables except the colour of the test number, so there was no reason to expect any inequality in performance. The only explanation is that the students were *seeing red*.

The research team wanted to verify their findings, so they tested their results in different experimental conditions, changing the type of test and the time of exposure. In the second experiment, conducted in Germany, the researchers manipulated the colour of the cover page and not the small number at the top of each page. They also changed the test itself. This time they gave an analogy test featuring questions such as '*legs* relates to *walk* like: 1. *tongue* to *mouth*, 2. *eyes* to *blink*, 3. *comb* to *hair*, or 4. *nose* to *face*'. (The correct answer, of course, is that you use your legs to walk just as you use your eyes to blink.)

Forty-six students participated in this experiment, and each received a binder with a cover page that contained twenty analogies to be solved in five minutes. The only difference among the groups was the colour of the cover page. For one group it was red, for the second group it was green, and for the third group it was white. Because the colour this time covered the entire first page, participants were exposed to it for a shorter time (only five seconds before being asked to turn the page) and only before the test (not during the test itself). Yet the results were very similar to those of the first experiment.

Again, those who had received a red cover page performed significantly worse than those with a green or white cover page. No

---

* The researchers took into consideration the general ability of the participants and made sure that this was not the cause of the differences between the groups.

difference was found between those who had green and those who had white cover pages.* The researchers conducted additional studies on a wide range of participants, who took both verbal and mathematical tests. Red consistently had a negative impact on test scores, regardless of the type of test or the identity of the test taker.

But what about the location of the testing? Well, it turns out that it doesn't matter where you take the test. The negative impact of the colour red on performance remained the same regardless of changes in environment. Instead of a lab setting, high school students took the analogy test in their classrooms as part of an 'IQ test'. This time, the students were tested in groups rather than one at a time. Still, their performances were remarkably influenced by simple manipulations of colour. The colour red showed itself to affect performance in virtually every instance, with high school and university students, with verbal and numerical tests, and in laboratories and other settings.

Participants were never aware of being manipulated by the researchers. The participants were even asked to guess the purpose of the study, and not one thought it had anything to do with the influence of colour. It seems that the colour red simply has a way of bullying its way into the human unconscious.

In further investigations, the researchers measured not how red influenced the students' performance but rather how it influenced their motivation. They found that seeing red evoked fear of failure and, consequently, avoidance behaviour, which means that the more afraid you are of failing, the more you try to avoid taking a test.

Elliot and his co-researchers came up with a creative way of measuring motivation in test taking.[4] Imagine two very different scenarios in which you are summoned to your boss's or superior's office: one

---

* In this experiment, too, the researchers took into consideration the general ability of the participants and made sure that this was not the cause of the differences between the groups.

is to get a raise, while the other is to explain why you failed to complete something on time. In both cases, when you get to the boss's office, the door is closed and you have to knock. In which of these two situations would you see yourself knocking more times? I think you'd agree that everyone is likely to knock more times when expecting good news.

To check out their assumption, researchers invited 67 students to a lab and told them they would be taking one of two tests: analogies or vocabulary. The experimenter provided a sample question from each of the tests, just to convince the students that this was what they would be doing. Then the researcher gave the students white binders, which he asked them to open and to read the name of the test printed on the first page. This was the test they believed they were going to take. The word *analogies* was printed in black ink on a red- or green-coloured rectangle.

After reading the name of the test that they thought they were going to take, participants were asked to go to the next lab – some 40 feet away – and take the test. The door to that lab was closed, and there was a Please Knock sign on the door. The students' knocks were recorded and counted. Those who saw the name of the test on a red background knocked fewer times than those who saw the name of the test on a green background. They were less motivated to take the test because of the colour red, which increased their anxiety and fear of failure.

How can something as simple as a colour so demonstrably affect performance and motivation? As for many issues in psychology, the answer is complex. Many potential emotional reactions can decrease performance and confidence. Red is associated with danger and can trigger nervousness or anxiety. It can provoke an anxious memory of any academic test that was marked up in red ink or stamped with the big old red rubber *F*. Such associations would understandably cause nervousness, which could lead to avoidance behaviour and lower performance.

The associations between red and danger are learned, but they may be rooted in our evolutionary predispositions. In the distant past, our reactions to certain colours proved adaptive, helping us to survive. Early in our childhood, when we see red stop signs and red traffic lights, for example, we have these tendencies reinforced as we learn to be alert to potential dangers.

The scientific findings about red impeding test performance should be taken seriously, particularly by teachers and educators. Simply by becoming aware of any subtle or subconscious factor that reduces success, including red's influence, we can begin to help students avoid or reduce its effects. For instance, a few years ago, the state government sent letters to 30 schools in Queensland, Australia, asking teachers not to use red pen to mark students' work since the colour is so aggressive. Significantly, they said the colour could harm students' psyches, which some people thought was over the top. After all, the studies you have just read about did not examine whether red is harmful to children's mental health. They did show very clearly that red has a negative influence on students' performance and decreased performance or failure might damage a child's psyche. It's simple enough for teachers to write their comments and indicate students' mistakes on tests, homework, or assignments in black pen or pencil or write them on a separate page in order to help reduce the association children make between the colour red and the danger of academic failure.

However, the main conclusions of these studies are not about the colour of the correcting pen but about red in the tests themselves. It is clear from these studies that teachers and educators should eliminate red from the test environment. Don't use red for the cover of the test booklet or write any instructions or numbers in red or use red in the colour of the bubbles that appear when you 'track changes' in Microsoft Word. Check your children's books and assignments to see if they contain a lot of red markings and bring these findings to their teachers' attention and to the attention of the textbook publishers. In the workplace and in everyday life, avoid writing instructions in red – employees or colleagues might find them harder to heed. This also holds true for manufacturers who supply instructions to board games as well as technical instructions for how to build a chair you bought in IKEA or how to operate that new food processor. Red is not the right colour for any of that, though, of course, it is the perfect universal signal in traffic lights and other signals of caution and danger.

Red affects us not only in the classroom. Two British researchers conducted a study that showed that martial artists and wrestlers won more often when they were wearing red outfits.[5] At first glance, this might seem to contradict the results of the test-taking studies just discussed, but stay with me here. The researchers examined four combat sports: tae kwon do, boxing, Greco-Roman wrestling and modern wrestling. In the 2004 Olympic Games, athletes were randomly assigned to wear either red or blue outfits or protective gear, yet for all four types of competitions, athletes who wore red won more fights. In another study, the same researchers investigated the success of English football teams from 1946–47 to 2001 and 2003 and correlated it with the colour of their shirts.[6] Teams that wore red shirts won more often than those with blue, yellow, orange, or white shirts.

It is possible that an athlete wearing red protective equipment or a red shirt experiences intensified emotions, which influence combat performance in a way dramatically different from the way they affect academic performance? Perhaps complex physical reactions to red – like adrenaline rushes or fight-or-flight responses – enhance wrestling ability but make it more difficult to sit down and focus on a verbal or mathematical test. Red might make you want to kill an equation, but that will do you no good on the test.

So these competition results are actually consistent with the previous test-taking findings. The athlete fighting the red-clad opponent sees the colour red – or danger – constantly coming at him. If a subtle red number on a test negatively affects the human subconscious, the red colour of a uniform might be much stronger. These data suggest not that the colour red enhances the performance of the wearer but rather that it increases anxiety in the opponent and thus hurts his ability to perform. However, it also could be that the person who wears the red outfit feels stronger, while the one facing him feels more vulnerable.

A third plausible interpretation of the results comes from three German researchers who argued that those who wear red win more often in competition not because of the influence of red on either of the athletes, but because of its influence on a third party: the referee.[7] They showed 42 referees videotape excerpts of five male competitors of similar ability performing tae kwon do. In each video, one athlete wore blue protective gear (on both head and torso), and the other wore red protective gear. In two video sequences, the videos were identical, but the uniform colours were reversed using digital graphics. Those who wore blue gear in the first sequence wore red gear in the second sequence, and those who wore red gear in the first sequence wore blue gear in the second sequence. Referees were asked to award points to each competitor after each video clip. Competitors who were dressed in red were awarded more points than those who were dressed in blue. Moreover, once the competitors who originally dressed in blue had their colour digitally transformed into red, they were awarded more points. The researchers suggested that these results demonstrate that the colour red indeed influences the referee. In reality, it probably influences everyone involved.

If red signals threaten us in certain situations, and as a result evoke avoidance behaviour, then it makes sense that this avoidance behaviour would interfere with cognitive and creative tasks. Avoidance behaviour might have a different influence on simple motor performance, however, so in two more experiments, researchers chose physical activities rather than mental tasks to examine the influence of red.[8] In one study, they asked participants to open a small clasp as wide as they could, but, before giving them that task, the researchers gave the participants a white paper with questions regarding their sex and age, and the participant number printed in either red or grey at the top of the page. Participants were asked to read loudly their participant number and then open the clasp. In another experiment, participants had to squeeze a handgrip as hard as they could for as long as the word *squeeze* appeared on the screen. *Squeeze* appeared on a red, blue, or green background.

In both experiments, red improved the performance of the subjects. They opened the clasp wider when they saw a red rather than a grey participant number and squeezed the handgrip harder when the instruction was on a red background as opposed to blue or green.

So is red good or bad for our performance? Does it help or does it make it worse? To answer, we have to distinguish between motor performance and cognitive performance as well as between complicated tasks and very simple tasks. In all cases red signals threat and evokes avoidance behaviour, and our reaction to this threat is to mobilise energy and use it to avoid the threat. Simple motor actions like gripping or squeezing or jumping are enhanced by this 'red alert'. In contrast, more complicated motor behaviours and cognitive tasks are impeded by a 'red alert'.

Regardless of the reason behind the impediments that red creates, the fact that it does create problems has direct implications for sports teams, schools, educators and test designers. The challenge that red presents to performance also extends into the virtual world. Several Romanian and Danish researchers found that in a popular video game genre of combat scenarios called first-person shooter, the red team usually has an advantage over the blue team.[9] Since wearing red affects physical performance, on the screen and in real life, sports coaches and video game designers should bear this in mind when choosing the uniforms of their teams or the options for their game play.

But context matters; red is also an extremely potent signal in another arena: sex and sexual behaviour.

5

The Lady in Red:
Red and Sexual Attraction

Eilat is a southern Israeli city located on the Red Sea. Its several beautiful beaches include Coral Beach, which is good for snorkelling and scuba diving. Every winter, I accompany my husband, an ophthalmologist, to a medical conference in Eilat. We usually go with another couple, good friends of ours. While our husbands audit lectures, my friend and I get to vacation. The winters in Eilat are warm, but often not warm enough to sit on the beach, so, especially in the afternoon, we go shopping. As the only city in Israel with no value-added tax, Eilat has attracted the trendiest, most elegant designer stores. We tourists and visitors can't resist the lower prices.

Last January, my friend and I were shopping and saw a red dress we both liked. When we tried it on, it looked really nice on both of us (we believed), and the price was unbeatable. We are good friends and don't mind having the same dress, so we each bought one. Back in the hotel, we told another friend about the bargains in that store, and she immediately went. But she came back with another dress, a black one, and said: 'I tried the red dress and it looked really great on me. But I didn't buy it. I bought a black dress instead, even though I have lots of black dresses at home and no red ones. But that dress was just too *red*.'

When I heard that, I started having doubts. I almost went to the store and exchanged my red dress for a black one. Perhaps I should have, because, although I have now had it for several months, I wear it far less often than my other dresses. I don't wear it on special occasions (it is not an evening dress), but I never wear it to work or to any of my lectures either. What did my other friend mean when she said it was too red? Why would she be more comfortable wearing the same dress in black than she was in red? What is it about this colour that made my friend reluctant to buy the dress, even though she thought she looked great in it? What is it about red that makes some women think it is too much, while others prefer it?

Part of the fun of being a professor is that sometimes I can pretend my graduate classes are small, informal focus groups. When I asked a class what colour is related to sex, 90 per cent answered 'red'. In red-light districts, sex is sold. Eve's red apple is a symbol of seduction. Valentine cards, symbolising romantic love, are often red. Red is considered an aphrodisiac, something that increases desire. In the movies, the sexy woman is usually dressed in red, from Marilyn Monroe in *Niagara* to Jessica Rabbit, iconic in her slinky red dress. In a scene in *American Beauty*, Lester (Kevin Spacey) dreams of his teenage temptress, Angela (Mena Suvari), lying naked on an enormous bed of red rose petals. The petals fall from the sky as dreamy chimes sound in the background. 'It's the weirdest thing,' Lester says in the voice-over. 'I feel like I've been in a coma for the past twenty years and I'm just now waking up.' Redness fills the shot.

Now let's see the scientific proof that red is associated with passion and sexuality. Might we perceive people differently because of the colour red? Do individuals consider those who wear red to be more beautiful; are they more attracted to them? In fact, red does all these things. Recently, Andrew Elliot and Daniela Niesta conducted a study to examine whether red really enhances men's attraction to women.[1] In the first experiment, researchers chose a black-and-white photo of the head and upper torso of a young adult woman with brown hair. They then showed the photo to two groups of male students, telling them they were studying first impressions of the opposite sex. The men were asked to look at the photo of the woman for five seconds before answering some questions. All the students saw the same photograph of the same woman for the same amount of time.

There was only one difference between the photos: half of the men saw the photo on a white background and the other half on a red background. The students were then asked to rate the attractiveness of the woman on a scale of 1 to 9. Men who saw the picture of the woman on a red background perceived her as more attractive than those who saw exactly the same picture on a white background.

In other words, *seeing red* influences personal attraction. We are strongly drawn to red, even though this effect is unconscious; the men had no idea that red was a factor in their decisions. They were all asked what they thought was affecting their perception most: the woman's facial expression, the way she was dressed, or the colour of the background. The students indicated that the colour had the *least* influence on their decision. But, after all, we don't always know what makes us tick.

The researchers were very thorough, conducting several more experiments to explore whether this effect of red could be universal. Participants in these experiments saw photos of different women with different physical traits, expressions and clothing. They saw photos of blonde women and brunette women; women who wore turtleneck sweaters and women who wore striped button-down shirts; women who were smiling and women who had a neutral expression. Sometimes the experimenters let the students study the photos for longer than five seconds. They compared the red background with grey, green and blue backgrounds, as well as with white. In one experiment, instead of colouring the background of the picture, the researchers tinted the woman's shirt red. They thought of nearly every way to challenge their findings, but the 'red effect' held fast.

Because 'attractive' and 'sexy' are not the same thing, although they are related, researchers also asked the participants to rate the extent to which they thought the woman was sexually desirable. The men also had to rate how much they would like to engage in several sexual activities with her, such as making out and having sexual intercourse. In one experiment, the participants were asked to rate the extent to which they wanted to ask this woman out and how much of a hundred dollars they would spend on her on a date. In addition, participants were asked to judge the woman on criteria not related to physical attractiveness and sex, including likeability and other positive qualities, such as how nice, honest, friendly, intelligent, and kind they believed she was.

Over and over and over again, the red effect on desire was consistent: participants perceived the woman in the picture with the red background as more attractive, more sexy and more desirable; and they claimed to have greater intentions to have sex with her, to date her, and to spend more money on her. The alluring effect of red was present with all types of women. Blonde or brunette, turtleneck or jacket, background or shirt colour, it didn't matter. Red affected the men's judgements about the woman in the picture, causing them to perceive her as more sexually attractive, completely without their awareness.

It is interesting, however, that red had no effect on the men's judgements of the woman's likeability or intelligence. Men did not perceive the woman with the red background as more (or less) nice, intelligent, or kind than the woman with a different-colour background. Red influenced only their judgements of the woman's attractiveness and their sexual attraction to her.

Together with two of my students,* I decided to replicate and expand this study. First, we wanted to see if red would have an effect on Israeli men similar to the one it had on the American men who had been tested. Israeli culture is very similar to American culture, and so red has similar associations. Replicating studies, especially across cultures, is important because it validates the findings, but we also had another goal: to test the influence of red on men's perceptions of women who were extremely attractive and of women who were below average in attractiveness. Yes, I know physical attractiveness is subjective, but there is some consensus about who is extremely attractive and who is unattractive. Media convey images of extraordinary beauties, but in the real world, not every woman is above average.

Elliot and his colleagues had studied women who were rated average, and, to determine who was considered average, they had conducted a pretest. They asked male participants (not those who later participated in their experiments with colour) to evaluate the attractiveness of women in photos on a scale of 1 to 9, where 1 was not at all attractive and 9 was extremely attractive. For their actual experiments, they chose only photos of women who had been given a score around 6. So their conclusions about the influence of the colour red apply only to moderately attractive women.

---

* Alon Valency and Gil Michaeli.

My students and I conducted a similar pretest. Based on its results, we chose photos of women who were perceived as moderately attractive, women who were perceived as below average in attractiveness, and women who were perceived as extremely attractive. We then presented 58 Israeli male students with photos of these women, some of whom were shown on a green background and some on a red. Participants answered three types of questions on a scale of 1 to 9. Two questions were about the perceived attractiveness of the woman ('How pretty is this woman?'; 'How attractive do you think she is?'), two questions were about the sexual attractiveness of the woman ('How sexually desirable do you find this woman?'), and two questions were about the sexual intentions of the man towards the woman ('On a scale of 1 to 9, how much would you like to have sex with the woman in the photo?'). In addition, we asked how likeable and intelligent the women seemed.

For the moderately attractive women, red had an effect on Israeli men similar to its effect on American men: Israeli men perceived moderately attractive women photographed against a red background as more attractive and more sexually desirable than women presented against a green background. In contrast, different results emerged for photos of women who were above or below average in attractiveness. When we isolated the attractive group and the unattractive group of women and then compared red and green backgrounds within each group, red had an effect *only* on the men's sexual desire and not on their perception of the women's attractiveness.

It should be noted that when we compared the attractive and unattractive women we found that irrespective of background colour, extremely attractive women were perceived as more attractive and more highly sexy than were women of below-average attractiveness. Men also reported being more eager to engage in sexual behaviour with the attractive women than with the unattractive women, regardless of background colour. However, a red background colour heightened their sexual desire for unattractive women. Similarly, they desired sex with attractive women presented against a red background more than they did with attractive women against a green background. Thus the across-the-board impact of red was felt in the middling zone of attractiveness. For the extreme groups the effect of red was limited to sexual desire.

These findings suggest that red can influence our desires even when it does not influence our conscious evaluations. Even when men consciously evaluate women as extremely sexy and attractive (or relatively unattractive and not sexy), they are unconsciously influenced by the colour red with regard to their willingness to have sex with the women.

While it's not news that women's physical appearance influences whether men find them attractive and sexy and how much men want to have sex with them, red also enhances – without our awareness – the desirability of women who are perceived as moderately attractive. The fact that red enhances the perceived attractiveness of moderately attractive women rather than the perceived attractiveness of those who are below or above average in attractiveness suggests that the effect of environmental factors is especially strong when other factors that influence our judgements and behaviour are relatively weak. When a woman is very attractive, this attractiveness is the most salient factor in judging how attractive and sexy she is, and the colour of the background matters less. This is called a *ceiling effect*. If, on the other hand, the woman is moderately attractive, then the environmental factors have a stronger influence, and in this case red is more influential. The more ambiguous the situation, the stronger the influence of the environmental factors. So if the woman is moderately attractive, the situation is more ambiguous and environmental factors play a bigger part.

Even in relatively clear-cut situations, environmental factors have an effect on our more automatic, less cognitive reactions. When the women were extremely attractive or unattractive, red did not influence how attractive or sexy they were perceived to be, but it still influenced how much the men wanted to have sex with them. This is consistent with other findings about the influence of environment. For instance, warm temperature affects our judgements of people who are not exhibiting particularly warm or cold behaviour. These results probably would not have been the same if the person had behaved in an extremely warm and friendly or extremely cold and unfriendly manner.

Recently Elliot and his colleagues examined whether the association between red and attraction is universal by conducting a study in a small, isolated rural community in Burkina Faso in West Africa.[2] They presented a black-and-white photo of an African woman, enclosed within either a blue or a red border, to 42 young men. The men were asked questions similar to those asked in previous studies conducted in the United States, Israel and Europe regarding women in photographs. The men rated the woman presented with the red border as more attractive than the one presented with the blue border, and wanted more strongly to meet her and to court her. However, unlike the results in the Western cultures, the finding here was that West African men who saw the woman in the red frame did not say they desired her more than did the men who saw the woman in the blue one. So the association between red and attraction exists in isolated cultures, proving the universal nature of this link. Yet the study also demonstrates that the association between red and sexual desirability is culture specific.

Elliot and his colleagues wanted to see if the colour red influences actual behaviour and not just intentions and evaluations.[3] Intentions often lead to actual behaviour, but not always. We have all had *intentions* of doing something – we meant to call someone, write something, go somewhere, change somehow – but did not follow through. The psychologists invited male students to participate in an experiment about communication. Actually, it was an experiment that faked communication. Researchers told the students that there was a woman in the other room and that they would be shown each other's photos: the participant would see the woman's image, and the woman the participant's image. But in fact there was no woman; the experimenter only showed each participant a photo of the head and torso of a woman who was moderately attractive. All participants received the same photo, but half received an image of the woman wearing a red T-shirt, while the other half saw a green T-shirt. This, again, was the only controlled difference in the experiment.

After showing the photo, the experimenter gave each participant a list of 24 questions and asked him to choose five that he wanted to ask the woman in the next room, which the experimenter would then take to the 'woman'. Some questions were not intimate or daring, such as 'Where were you born?' Some were moderate, and asked the woman where she usually hangs out. And some were quite daring, such as 'What should a guy do in order to get your attention if he sees you in a bar?' The results showed that the participants who saw the woman in a red shirt asked her more intimate questions than did the participants who saw the same photo but with a green shirt.

The psychologists conducted a second experiment in which they showed each participant a photo of the same woman, but some saw her in a red shirt and some in a blue shirt. Supposedly, the students would meet her in the next room. After seeing the photo, participants were asked to go to the other room to talk with the woman, who would arrive after they were seated. Each participant was to take a chair and position it across from her empty chair. Again, there was no woman, but the experimenters measured the distance the men put between the chairs, and the results were impressively significant. Participants sat closer to the empty chair after seeing the photo of the woman in the red shirt than after seeing the one of the woman in blue. The romantic intentions of the men did indeed translate into intimate behaviour.

A number of studies have sought to examine this link between red and attraction in real-life situations. One study checked to see whether waitresses who wore red were tipped more.[4] For six weeks, experimenters observed eleven young waitresses working in five different restaurants in France. The waitresses did not know the purpose or hypothesis of the experiment but were instructed each day which colour T-shirt to wear – red, black, white, yellow, blue, or green. The experimenters recorded the tips of 722 customers, males and females, who sat alone at a table.

The men (but not the women) tipped the waitresses who wore red more than those who wore any other colour. The possibility exists, however, that although the waitresses were unaware of the purpose of the study, they nevertheless behaved differently when they wore red. We need new studies to investigate this question.

In another study, one of these researchers examined whether a red T-shirt influenced drivers to stop for hitchhikers.[5] Five young women wore different-colour T-shirts and were asked to hitchhike and count the number of drivers who stopped for them. As in the waitress study, male drivers stopped more frequently when a woman was wearing a red T-shirt. Female drivers did not.

It seems that in real-life situations men are more attracted to women who wear red, even a simple T-shirt, than to women who wear any other colour.

The attractiveness of red is common to many other primates. Recently a group of researchers presented male rhesus macaques with various faces of females on a computer screen.[6] Some of the faces were pale, and some were red. The researchers measured the time that the male monkeys spent gazing at each face. They found that the males gazed longer at red faces than at pale ones and concluded that the colour red is a factor in attraction. This experiment is especially interesting because this behaviour of the monkeys was studied not in the wild but in a controlled setting, the same way that we psychologists study human beings. In fact, rhesus macaques are often used in studies because they are our close relatives.

Red-Letter Days

Red connects with strong instincts and powerful emotions. In Nathaniel Hawthorne's classic novel *The Scarlet Letter*, which takes place in a seventeenth-century Puritan village, Hester Prynne bears a child out of wedlock and is required to wear a piece of red cloth in the shape of the letter *A* every day. Why red? Literature classes have discussed the significance of this colour choice for over a hundred years. Does it represent blood? Sin? The danger she poses to the community?

As this famous story suggests, and as we know from experience and from literature and film, red is a sexy colour. Temptresses, the libertine Jezebels of literature, are usually depicted wearing red. Scarlett O'Hara's name itself is red. Yet I doubt that most of us would have thought that simply changing the colour behind a picture of a woman would strongly influence men's judgements of the woman and influence their intentions towards her. Of course, the colours around you (even red) are not the ultimate factor in your choices or behaviours, just one of many. But the colour red is worthy of respect. It is a serious influence, and being mindful of it will help you work with its effects.

In everyday life, in the eternal question of what to wear if you are a woman and you want to look sexy, red is your scientifically approved go-to colour. A red blouse or a red hat will make you stand out in a crowd, but so will a less conspicuous red item, such as a scarf, a ribbon, lipstick, or even a red T-shirt over blue jeans. Red can be overused, like adding too much spice to food. It's also helpful to know when *not* to wear red, when such a signal is inappropriate. When you are planning to go to any kind of meeting, whether business, social, or romantic, you might well ask yourself, 'How do I want to be perceived?' and decide accordingly on the colour of your outfit. Then again, you might decide that you don't really much care how you are perceived and wear only what you like and what makes you feel comfortable. Maybe the poets were almost onto something: roses *are* red, violets *are* blue … but 'tis *colour itself* my mind loves about you.

Well-Red Men

Does red enhance the desirability of men to women? Sexy men are not necessarily portrayed wearing red shirts. The songs and movies are about a 'lady in red' and a 'woman in red'. There is no 'man in red'.

Red is associated not only with sex but also with dominance, especially in the animal world. Studies with various types of animals have shown that red in males signals dominance, which is preferred by females for mating. When my friends and I were kids and went to the zoo, we thought the red rumps of some of the baboons were hilarious, but the red backside is serious; males, especially alpha males (and not females), display it as a symbol of status. Researchers from the United Kingdom found that the red colour on the face, rump and genitalia of male mandrills is a sign of dominance.[7] When two males with similar red colour encountered each other, there were more fights and aggressive behaviour. When one of the males exhibited a stronger red colour, however, he was clearly more dominant, and the less dominant male avoided him.

Red signals dominance in other types of animals too. In Sydney,

Australia, researchers found that redheaded male morphs of the colour-polymorphic Gouldian finch population are always the dominant birds.[8] They are more dominant and aggressive than black-headed and yellow-headed morphs. Even artificial red signals dominance and influences the behaviour of zebra finches, common birds in Australia. Researchers arbitrarily placed red or green bands on the legs of zebra finches and found that those with the red bands were more dominant.[9] Animal studies have also shown that females prefer dominant red males. For example, the three-spined stickleback fish appears red during breeding season. Researchers found that the females preferred males with more intense red colour.[10]

Two British researchers investigated whether red conveyed dominance in inanimate objects.[11] They presented participants with blue and red circles and asked them to indicate which shape appeared to be more dominant. This might seem a strange question. How can shapes look dominant? However, when participants had to choose, they answered that the red circle was more dominant. The word *dominant,* and the concept it represents, immediately and without their awareness pointed their minds towards red.

Dominance is considered a stereotypically masculine characteristic, and many studies have shown that women like dominant men and men with higher status. Elliot and Niesta with their colleagues asked this question: 'If red is associated with dominance and status, and if women prefer men with higher status, is it possible that women will find a man wearing a red item more attractive?'[12] They conducted seven experiments on the effect of red on women's perception of men. The first five experiments were very similar to those I described earlier, which examined the effect of red on men's perception of women. This time, however, the participants were women who saw photos of men.

The researchers presented female students with black-and-white photos of a man on a red, white, or grey background. The researchers asked the women to rate how attractive they perceived the man to be and how sexually attracted they were to the man. Women who saw the photo of the man on a red background perceived him as more attractive and as more sexually desirable than did women who saw the same photo on a white or grey background. Similar results were found when, instead of the background, the researchers manipulated shirt colour. Women were asked to judge a man wearing a red shirt or a green shirt. And wouldn't you know it? The man with the red shirt was perceived as more attractive and desirable.

The researchers went one step further to examine what it is in the colour red that affects women's judgements of men. They once again presented female students with a photo of a man. As in the previous studies, all participants saw the same photo, but half saw the man wearing a red shirt and the other half a grey shirt. This time, they were asked to evaluate the status of the man and his status potential, that is, whether he had a high potential to succeed in the future and to earn a lot. The findings are extraordinary. Women who saw the man with the red shirt believed he had a higher status and a higher potential for status and success. In other words, exactly the same man was perceived as higher in status just because he wore a red shirt.

These experiments clearly demonstrate that the colour red has a strong influence on women's perception of men's attractiveness and plays an important part in the attraction between the sexes. Red signals a higher status, and higher status in men makes them more attractive and sexually desirable. It seems that on women red symbolises sex and consequently attracts men, and on men it symbolises dominance and status and attracts women. Thus, red influences attraction in both sexes, but for different reasons. However, we need more studies to fully understand this phenomenon.

Red may bestow status on women too. Elliot and Niesta, who

conducted the studies on men's perceptions of women, did not examine the possibility that red might be associated with status in women as well. We should therefore ask whether it is possible that red signals dominance and higher status not only in the eyes of women who are judging men but also in the eyes of men who are judging women. Elliot and his colleagues have noted that in the animal world red signals status in males, but no study has directly asked whether red in women also signals status, and whether high status in women attracts men. So, we need more studies to fully understand this phenomenon too.

Men can easily apply these findings by wearing something red in social interactions and business meetings. Wearing a red tie or a red shirt may confer just enough status in a professional setting or on a date to lead to success.

Every day, people pitch their ideas to potential investors, to colleagues, to clients, and in job interviews. Naturally, they all put serious thought into the best way to present an idea, as well as what to wear. Clothing is part of the presentation. The results of the studies described here suggest that a red tie or another subtle red item would be positively influential. Of course a red suit would have adverse effects – it would be too loud and detract from the presentation. However, when situations are not clear-cut and investors or clients may feel they are taking a certain risk, colour will play a part in conveying the authority of the presenter.

Male politicians often wear a red tie when they want to convince people to vote for them or to believe in them. They or their advisers must have heard of market research that demonstrates the influence of the colour red on our perceptions and behaviours, or they have sensed the association of red with power, authority and dominance. In the marketing world, the colour red influences price perceptions. For example, male consumers perceived greater savings when the prices were written in red, as compared with black.[13]

The impact of clothing is well known and borne out by numerous studies. A few examples: teaching assistants who wear formal clothes are perceived as more competent than those who wear less formal clothes;[14] women in prestigious jobs who wear sexy clothes are perceived as less competent than those who dress more conservatively;[15] customers believe they will be given higher-quality service and exhibit stronger purchasing intentions when customer service agents are dressed appropriately.[16]

Not only are the perceptions and judgements of others affected by the clothes we wear but so is our own behaviour. Recently researchers demonstrated that subjects who wore white lab coats performed better on cognitive tasks that demanded selective attention than did those who wore regular clothes.[17] Moreover, the researchers found this effect held true only when the white coat resembled a doctor's coat rather than a painter's coat.

I was recently watching on TV two candidates – a man and a woman – running to head one of Israel's political parties. The man wore a dark suit with a red tie; the woman's outfit had no red in it. In videos of past interviews, he had not worn a red tie except on election day, when he wanted most to convey confidence, dominance and the potential for future success. So the candidate had been either studying his psychology or watching American politicians. He beat the female candidate by a large margin. No doubt, gender stereotypes played a role. It would be interesting to examine the best colour for female politicians to wear, since most likely they should not wear red.

We take for granted that most of us can see colour. The fact that our brains can even receive such signals is amazing. Human beings are only one of the millions of species on this planet who need vision to survive, yet our eyes have red-green receptors that allow us to experience the rich quality of the light around us. It may seem arbitrary, but the specific wavelengths we sense as redness (approximately 630 to 740 nanometres) beam with certain associations. Red explodes in our minds, signalling passion, danger, mating and dominance. We react to this colour strongly and automatically. Fortunately, with knowledge and awareness, we can regulate our responses and become mindful of environmental triggers that aim to mislead us.

The entertainment and marketing industries know how to use colours to great effect. Take note of the sports uniforms you see and the clothes your friends wear at a party. Notice what colours you yourself choose to wear. Check out the backgrounds of billboards and magazine advertisements, the light in restaurants and art galleries. Be aware that you may feel suddenly, subtly different when you are in the presence of red. By understanding the power of red, you can understand a bit more about human behaviour – and share in that power of red.

6

In Contrast:
Separating the Light from the Darkness

A woman doesn't wear a white dress to a wedding unless she's the bride. Most of us know that this is just not something you do. But there are certain occasions on which you are *supposed* to wear white. The Jewish holiday Shavuot is one of them. Although this holiday may not be well known among secular Jews around the world, it is celebrated widely in Israel and has its own special traditions. For example, people eat only dairy products (no meat). Many people will also wear white. All around Israel you see children, usually carrying bags of fruit, dressed all in white.

About three years ago, my husband and I attended a Shavuot party thrown by a couple we've known for many years. The host was an economist and a stockbroker, and his guests were mostly economists, businessmen, politicians and lawyers, all highly esteemed in Israel. It was our first time attending the party, and we were late arriving.

About 150 guests were already mingling in the spacious garden. I was
wearing a classic 'little black dress' (it was a party, after all), but, to
my horror, the first thing I noticed as we walked into the garden was
that everybody – *everybody* – was wearing white. I was the opposite of
fashionably late.

I must have figured the Shavuot custom was for schoolchildren
only, because I hadn't given any thought to my dress. But the women
were all in white dresses, or a white blouse with white trousers or
white skirt, and the men were in white shirts and trousers. In the
midst of such a white-out, I felt terribly self-conscious in my black
dress, and felt the need to explain myself. 'Nobody warned me!' I
insisted. Eventually I started socialising, greeting some people I knew.
Israel is a small country, and many of the businessmen, media figures
and politicians were familiar to me. Some I knew personally, while
others were faces I knew from TV and newspapers.

After overcoming my embarrassment at being one of the two
off-colour guests (the other was my husband), I started to enjoy the
party. Everyone seemed so pleasant! I clearly remember thinking, and
later telling a friend, that most of the people, including the rather
sharklike politicians and hard-nosed businessmen, seemed particularly
nice. Was it the holiday spirit? Was it something about the kindness
of the hosts? Maybe. But could it have also been that I perceived the
guests as nicer simply because they were all wearing white? Does seeing white influence our state of mind and judgement?

White and black symbolise opposite concepts. White symbolises
goodness – purity, morality, virtue and cleanliness – and dark symbolises evil. In the Book of Isaiah, it is written, '"Come now, let us
reason together," says the Lord. "Though your sins are like scarlet,
they shall be as white as snow"' (1:18). Many cultural traditions use
white for things other than bridal dresses. The ancient Greeks wore
white when they went to sleep, believing that this would give them

pleasant dreams. Angels are usually portrayed as dressed in white; the symbol of peace is a white dove; a white flag indicates truce. In fairy tales, white knights on white horses rescue young girls. We commonly use metaphors such as *pure as snow* and *whiter than white*, all of which indicate good attributes.

White can also connote spirituality. Mother Teresa of Calcutta chose to wear a white sari with blue stripes to embody caring and compassion. Mahatma Gandhi also always wore white, to represent the tradition of self-sufficiency in his homespun cloth as well as peace in his non-violent resistance to British rule. Black, on the other hand, symbolises negativity, evil and contamination. Metaphors such as *black days, blacklist, black book, black cloud, black sheep* and *black market,* as well as common words such as *blackmail,* all have negative connotations. Witches are often portrayed wearing black, and people who practise witchcraft (a so-called dark art) wear black. Evil characters such as Darth Vader and Voldemort are clad in black, as was Maleficent, the mistress of all evil in *Sleeping Beauty.* Often a devil personified is shown wearing black, even when it is Prada, as in Lauren Weisberger's 2003 novel and the movie of three years later starring Meryl Streep and Anne Hathaway.

Of course, black can also be associated with elegance. Many women wear black dresses for formal events, but in an artistic context, black usually symbolises wickedness. Take Darren Aronofsky's popular film *Black Swan,* for example. Natalie Portman portrayed Nina and won an Oscar for her role as a dancer in a New York ballet company who struggles to get the lead in *Swan Lake.* In this fictitious production of the classical ballet, the white swan represents innocence and purity, and her lustful twin, the black swan, sexuality and dangerous, dark impulses. Nina has to cope with these opposite forces in her own soul. When she auditions, the choreographer claims that she is suited only for the role of the white swan, since she is not worldly enough and lacks the necessary passion to be the black swan. When she convinces him otherwise, demonstrating her dark sensuality, Nina gets the role of the black swan. Through its tragic end, the movie deals with these opposites: the purity and restraint represented by the colour white, and the aggression and primal power represented by the colour black.

As in the Book of Genesis, the distinction between light and dark is the first indication of being and consciousness. God brings light out of chaos and 'darkness ... upon the face of the deep.' 'And God said, Let there be light: and there was light.' Light is also the first experience of an infant upon leaving his mother's womb – from darkness to a flood of light. When the infant closes his eyes, he is enveloped in darkness. But when he reopens his eyes – light!

Black and white are no ordinary colours. In fact, according to scientists, black is the complete absence of light, and so symbolises darkness. The darker something is, the more it appears black. White, on the other hand, is the presence of light that stimulates all three types of cone cells in the eye. Mixing any colour with white makes it appear lighter. Many researchers study these related phenomena together and even use the terms interchangeably, referring to the stimuli as dark and black, light and white.

The Sons of Light Against the Sons of Darkness

In 1954, an ad in *The Wall Street Journal* announced the sale of a biblical manuscript written over two thousand years ago. While it did not draw much attention at the time, it was for the Dead Sea Scrolls, manuscripts written on papyrus and preserved in clay jars. Found in 1947 in a Qumran cave by three Bedouin shepherds, and widely considered one of the most important archaeological discoveries in history, the Dead Sea Scrolls are the oldest known copies of what

Christians consider the Old Testament and Jews call the Bible. They shed light on the early historical period before the Common Era, or the birth of Jesus, and on Judeo-Christian theology.

One of the first scrolls found is called *The War of the Sons of Light Against the Sons of Darkness* and is known informally as the War Scroll. Acquired for the Hebrew University in Jerusalem, it contains a prophecy that describes a coming war between the good people of the world, who are the congregation of God, and the evil people, the people of the enemy nations. The 'sons of light' are the various tribes of Israel, while the 'sons of darkness', or evil people, are various other peoples, including the Edomites, Amalekites, Hittites and Moabites. The war, described in great detail, lasts for 40 years and ends with the victory of the sons of light.

These associations of light and goodness, dark and evil, are ancient. Our minds make them automatically and instinctually. Metaphors such as *seeing the light* and the *light at the end of the tunnel* symbolise good things. Like light, brightness is also used to symbolise good things. We look on the *bright side,* speak of having a *bright future,* and believe we are better and more productive when we wake up *bright and early*. On the other hand, we use metaphors such as *the Dark Ages* to refer to a historical period of stagnation and decline and point out a person's *dark side* to warn about her character and behaviour. *Dark past, dark secret* and *forces of darkness* are all negative. In the Star Wars series, the Force also has its Dark Side.

The poet John Milton described hell in his epic poem *Paradise Lost* as 'no light, but rather darkness visible', a phrase that novelist William Styron borrowed for his memoir of suffering from severe depression, *Darkness Visible: A Memoir of Madness*. Psychoanalyst and philosopher Julia Kristeva wrote about depression and melancholia in her book *Black Sun*. My late friend Professor Norman Endler, a distinguished psychologist and researcher from York University in Canada, wrote a book called *Holiday of Darkness*, in which he described his depression and how it affected his life and his family. These titles show the complexity of negative psychological states – the paradox of holding goodness and darkness within us.

In everyday life we use metaphors that relate white, bright and light to positive states and things, and black and dark to negative, frightening and immoral acts and things. The question is: Are these simply figures of speech? Or do dark or black stimuli actually evoke negative emotions, while bright and white stimuli evoke positive emotions? How strong and instinctive are these associations between white and good, and black and evil, and might these ingrained associations influence the course of our lives by affecting our judgement and behaviour? Is it really possible that I perceived the people at that Shavuot party as being kinder because they were all dressed in white?

Several researchers have investigated these questions using what is called the *Stroop effect*. The Stroop effect refers to incongruence between the meaning of a word and the colour of the font in which that word is printed. In classic Stroop tests, participants read the names of colours, but the letters appear in a colour different from the colour that they name. For example, the word *green* is printed in red ink, rather than in green ink, and the word *yellow* is written in blue.

Participants are asked to name the colour of the ink, and their response time is measured. If the word is *table*, for example, and *table* is printed in red, you will have no difficulty saying 'red'. However, if the word is *green* and it's printed in red, you will have more difficulty saying 'red', because the colour of the ink (red), is incongruent with what you read (*green*). In this case, the meaning of the word (*green*) interferes with the colour of the word (red). You are actually receiving contradictory information, so your mind takes longer to perform this task. This confusion is the Stroop effect at work.

Researchers have adapted the idea of the Stroop effect to test metaphors. Instead of using incongruent colour names and ink colours, they showed participants positive and negative words printed in bright or dark colours.[1] Participants were presented with positive words such as *generous, brave, faith, gentle, hero, kiss, love, devotion, mature* and *loyal*, and negative words such as *cruel, crime, bitter, cancer, fraud, nasty, liar, poison, rude* and *unfair*, and they were asked to indicate whether each word was positive or negative. The researchers varied the brightness of the letters so that some of the words were bright and white, while others were dark and black. Then they measured how long it took participants to categorise the words as positive or negative. The faster the participants answered, the easier the task was assumed to have been. Researchers also measured how accurate the participants were, especially when they were told to answer as quickly as possible.

If metaphorical brightness is indeed related to positivity and darkness to negativity, then a dark positive word is metaphorically incongruent. The dark tint would interfere with the positive meaning of the word. A person who sees a positive word printed in dark ink receives two contradictory pieces of information. On the one hand, dark is negative, but, on the other hand, the word is positive. If positivity is automatically and instinctively associated with brightness and negativity with darkness, then the task should be more time-consuming when a positive word is dark and a negative word bright.

Indeed, it was much easier for participants to correctly categorise the words as positive when they were bright and as negative when they were dark. It took longer to categorise the words when they were bright but negative, or dark but positive. Participants were also less accurate when the positive words were dark and the negative words were bright, especially when they were pressed to answer quickly. These findings suggest that we instinctively associate brightness with positivity, white with good, dark with bad, and black with evil.

This effect is surprisingly strong. A group of Dutch researchers recently investigated these same associations, but in a different way from their American colleagues.[2] Their experiment was ostensibly to see if the participants could translate certain Dutch words into Chinese (even though the participants did not speak Chinese). The researchers presented the participants with words in Dutch (their mother tongue), some of which were negative and some of which were positive. Under each word they presented two Chinese ideo-graphs, one black and one white, and the participants had to choose which of the two ideographs was the correct translation of the Dutch word. The participants chose white ideographs more often when the word was positive and black ideographs when the word was negative. Remember, the participants had no knowledge of Chinese; they were just guessing.

These experiments' strong results suggest that we make judgements about the positivity or negativity of people and events based on seemingly irrelevant factors, such as the colours white and black. A person wearing white clothes is likely to be perceived more positively than a person wearing black clothes. Perhaps I was naturally inclined to enjoy the all-white Shavuot party, but on the flip side, I hate to think of how the other guests must have viewed me, a black swan in a sea of white.

After completing my PhD at Tel Aviv University, I went with my husband and three-year-old daughter to Cambridge, Massachusetts, where I did my postdoctorate studies at Harvard University while my husband did research at MIT. In Tel Aviv, our home town, we had lived in a bright house with big windows and white walls. The first apartment we rented in Cambridge, however, had small windows, and walls painted a dark grey. I remember those first months in Cambridge as really difficult. Everything seemed negative to me, but I figured that this feeling was normal, attributing it to loneliness because I was in an unfamiliar place where I knew hardly anyone. A year later, we moved to another apartment, which was smaller but much brighter and with big windows. All of a sudden, I started thinking how great Cambridge was and how happy I was that we had moved there. I attributed this change in my feelings to the time that had passed, allowing me to get used to my new home, to make my way around, and to find friends. Looking back, however, I now believe my first months spent in a relatively dark apartment influenced my emotions and judgements. In fact, we ended up loving our time in Cambridge so much that seven years later, we returned for another year, when I taught in the Psychology Department at Harvard. That second time around we made sure to choose a bright apartment from the start. As a result, Cambridge looked beautiful and I was very happy there.

Black Eyes: Black and Destructive Behaviour

More than twenty years ago, two researchers from Cornell University, Mark G. Frank and Thomas Gilovich, wanted to examine whether the black-evil and white-good associations influence not just our judgements but also our everyday actions.[3] They showed participants black and white uniforms and found that people perceived the black uniforms as meaner and more aggressive than they perceived the white uniforms. They then examined fifteen years of penalty records of professional teams from the National Football League and the National Hockey League in the United States. They found that teams wearing black uniforms were penalised more often than teams wearing other colours.

It is interesting, but also troublesome, that these findings represent an unconscious bias. They offend our sense of fairness. The numbers might be explained in various ways, however. Perhaps those who wear black uniforms behave more aggressively and deserve to be penalised more often. Perhaps the coaches and general managers who chose black uniforms also selected more aggressive players to create a more aggressive team. To further investigate these potential causes, Frank and Gilovich conducted another experiment.

In this clever study, the researchers prepared two nearly identical videos of football plays with the only difference being that in one version the players wore white uniforms and in the other, black. The researchers showed the videos to two groups: students who were college football fans and professional football referees. Both groups were asked how likely they would be to penalise the team and how aggressively the team was playing. The results were astonishing. Both the college students and the professional referees said that they would penalise the team wearing black uniforms more often than the team wearing white. Remember, the game sequences were identical; the only thing that changed was the colour of the uniforms. These results clearly demonstrate that the black uniform colour influenced the referees, leading them to perceive those who wear black uniforms as more aggressive.

But are these results really so black and white? To examine whether wearing a black uniform influences not only the perceptions of the referees but also the actual behaviour of those who wear that colour, the researchers devised another experiment. Students from Cornell University were grouped in threes and told that another group was waiting in a separate room. Each 'team' was given a list of twelve available games, and the participants were asked to choose five games in which to compete against the other group. The games varied in aggressiveness. Some were quite aggressive, such as human 'cock-fighting', in which one person sits on the shoulders of another and tries to knock down the opposing team members. Some games were completely tame, such as stacking blocks. Participants were told that because each person had chosen a different game, they would now have to arrive at a consensus on which games they would play as a group. The experimenter asked them to wear uniforms so that they would really feel like a group while they made their decision and gave them either white or black uniforms. It turned out that those who were given black uniforms chose more aggressive games than those who wore white. Yet when participants did not wear uniforms, there was no difference between the two groups. It seems as though just the act of wearing the black uniform increased the group's willingness to engage in aggressive games.

In 2012, a group of researchers wanted to expand on Frank and Gilovich's first study on the effect of colour on penalties in professional sports leagues, so they analysed penalties in the National Hockey League with a considerably larger sample size: the last 25 seasons before 2010.[4] Unlike Frank and Gilovich, who focused only on the difference between black and colour jerseys, they also examined the difference between white and colour jerseys. They found similar results regarding the black jerseys: more penalties were given when players were wearing black jerseys than when they were wearing other colours. It is interesting to note that this was true only for aggressive penalties, such as elbowing and boarding, and not for non-aggressive technical infractions, such as being offside or having too many men on the ice. The researchers also found that wearing white jerseys led to fewer penalties. In short, white was linked to less aggressive behaviour and black to more aggressive behaviour, at least as measured by the penalties.

These results suggest that the negative metaphors of black and the positive ones of white affect not only our judgements and evaluations but also our behaviour. Wearing black might increase our aggressive behaviour and also influence how we are judged by others. The fact that all the guests at the Shavuot party were wearing white might have affected their own behaviour. They might really and truly have been behaving more nicely.

As Frank and Gilovich noted, context matters. In aggressive, competitive situations, black is associated with aggression and competitiveness. Uniforms are related to group identity and thus are not the same as regular clothes. But as soon as we suit up, we invite certain associations, whether in a sports uniform or in an official uniform, a police or military uniform, formal or black-tie attire.

Why don't we associate white with negatives and black with positives? How did we develop the universal associations of bright-positive and dark-negative? The answer, many scientists believe, is that we inherited these links over the course of our evolution as a species and they are reinforced by our individual experiences. The link between positivity and brightness, for example, may be embodied in our very biology. The fact is that we are diurnal, not nocturnal, creatures. We live by day, functioning better in the light, where we can see our surroundings. Life is less dangerous in the sunlight. We come into the world primed for light. Throughout our lives, we tend to experience things as better and more positive while in the light. Living by day conveys a survival advantage that we share with others.

Evolution established the link between darkness and danger, but our childhood experiences reinforce it. Even if children do not show any specific signs of fear of darkness, most children do not prefer the dark. My own children always wanted me to leave their bedroom doors open for a sliver of light. The associations between darkness and bad things begin at the sensory level, when children are lying in bed. In darkness, they feel alone and apart, scared and vulnerable. Upon closing his eyes, an infant sees darkness, but when he opens his eyes again he sees the light. Put yourself in the place of the baby and close your eyes for a full 30 seconds. How did it feel? How did your experience of your environment change? Did your posture or orientation shift? In the dark, we lose contact with our surroundings and are in a vulnerable position; someone could sneak up on us. In the light, on the other hand, we feel more in control; it is easier to adapt our behaviour to fit in with others around us and to navigate our environment.

Darkness represents an undifferentiated chaos and disorder – even death. In the light, we are in touch with the world. This deep-seated emotional connection is poignantly illustrated in the last words of Goethe, the celebrated German poet and writer. 'More light,' he said, asking his attendant to open the shutters covering the window.

Dim the Lights: Positivity, Negativity, and the Perception of Physical Brightness

Brightness is related to positive judgements, but is it possible that it can also work the other way around? Might our positive or negative judgements and emotions influence our perceptions of physical brightness? For example, will the same object or person look brighter when our own mood is bright and positive?

We perceive physical brightness from the amount of light that comes from a certain object. The more light that comes from an object, the brighter it appears. But our perception of brightness can be subjective and depend on context. For example, the brightness of the objects around us and the brightness of the background affect how we perceive the brightness or darkness of a particular object.

Although in reality the same amount of light might come from two objects, our physical sensation of them can be affected by other factors. This is a well-known phenomenon that every photographer comes to understand.

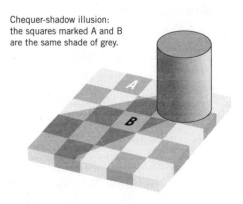

Chequer-shadow illusion: the squares marked A and B are the same shade of grey.

It is hard to believe, but squares A and B are the same shade of grey.* Square A is on a light background, and square B is on a dark background. If you are sceptical, cover the squares that surround squares A and B and examine them again.

Several researchers have examined the possibility that the brightness of an object is influenced by psychological factors such as judgements, emotions, and positive and negative associations. The same object may look brighter after we have been exposed to positive words and darker after we have been exposed to negative words.

In one experiment, participants wore headphones while 100 words, 50 positive and 50 negative, appeared on the screen, one at a time.[5] Participants had to declare whether the word they were

---

* http://persci.mit.edu/gallery/checkershadow.

seeing was positive or negative. They were told that after each word they would also see on the screen either a bright square or a dark square. Participants had to indicate whether that square was the darker or the brighter one. In fact, there was only one square. After evaluating negative words, participants more often believed that they saw the 'darker square', while after evaluating the positive words, participants believed more often that they saw the 'brighter square'. Yet remember, they always saw exactly the same square.

In another experiment, the same researchers presented participants with positive and negative words that appeared on the screen in differing degrees of brightness. Participants evaluated each word as positive or negative and then were shown five squares that differed in gradations of darkness (on a spectrum from white to black). They had to choose the square that matched the colour of the word. For instance, participants were presented with positive words such as *clean, champion, hero, polite* and *nurse,* and negative words such as *vulgar, bitter, crooked, diseased* and *enemy.* As in the previous study, the perception of physical brightness depended on the positivity or negativity of the meaning of the word. Participants more frequently chose a lighter shade for positive words than for negative words, even though there were bright and dark words in both positive and negative categories.

Researchers examined metaphors such as *bright smile* by studying whether smiling faces are indeed perceived as physically brighter, in terms of light strength, compared with frowning faces.[6] In several experiments, the researchers found that the metaphor *bright smile* is not just a figure of speech; smiling faces presented in different colours and in different formats were perceived as physically brighter than frowning faces.

In a recent study participants were asked to recall and describe an unethical or ethical behaviour from their past, then asked to judge the brightness of the room on a seven-point scale.[7] Those who recalled an unethical deed rated the room as darker than those who recalled an ethical deed. In a second study participants were similarly asked to recall and describe an ethical or unethical deed but then asked to state their preferences for light-related products – a flashlight, a candle and a lamp – and neutral products: crackers, an apple and a jug. Those who recalled an unethical deed showed greater preference for the light-related products than those who recalled an ethical behaviour.

Amazingly, all these findings demonstrate that the perception of brightness or darkness depends not only on the objective brightness of that stimulus, which is the amount of light coming from it, but also on our psychological and moral evaluations. Our eyes see something, but our minds change it according to our bias, which is evident in our metaphors. The amount of light coming from two different objects may be exactly the same, but if one is negative (e.g. a gun) and the other one is neutral or positive (e.g. a dark-coloured flower, such as a pansy), the negative object will look darker than the positive one. Making this distinction is automatic and instinctive. When we judge a person as bad, we probably perceive his surroundings as being darker too. When we have a good, positive experience, we perceive that day as brighter. These relationships between brightness and positivity and darkness and negativity go both ways: bright things are perceived as more positive, and positive things are perceived as brighter. Similarly, darker things are perceived as negative, and negative things are perceived as darker.

Like a Thief in the Night

In a study provocatively titled 'The Colour of Sin', two researchers focused on a specific aspect of negativity: immorality.[8] They also used the Stroop effect, but in a different way. Participants were asked to read immoral and moral words, such as *abusive, cheat, sin, evil, honesty, freedom, helping* and *justice,* printed in black or white. However, unlike participants in previous studies, who were asked to indicate whether words were positive or negative, the participants here were asked to name the colour that the words were printed in – black or white. Participants identified the colours of moral words, such as *honesty* and *kind,* faster when they were printed in white, and the colours of immoral words, such as *cruel* and *cheat,* faster when they were printed in black. We automatically and instinctively associate immorality with black and morality with white. This association may also influence our moral or immoral behaviour in the real world.

It is a fact that more crimes are committed at night than during the day. The same street is usually safer in daylight than in the dark. To protect ourselves, we are told not to park our cars in remote places at night, not to walk alone at night, and not to go to the ATM machine at 2.00 a.m. All these warnings assume that at night we have to take additional precautions. A simple way to decrease criminal activity and reduce fears of crime has been to increase street lighting at night. Of course, it is easier for a criminal to act in the dark, where he's less conspicuous. But people might also be more inclined to behave immorally in the dark even when the darkness is not related to being noticed or discovered and does not facilitate the immoral behaviour in any practical way. In other words, it is possible that the metaphorical association between darkness and immoral behaviour affects crime statistics.

A group of researchers invited college students to participate in an experiment examining this possibility.[9] They divided the students into two groups: one group sat in a room full of light (with twelve fluorescent lights), while the other group sat in a dim room (with only four fluorescent lights). All the students received twenty matrices, and for each matrix they were asked to find two numbers that added up to ten. The students were given five minutes to complete this task and received 50 cents for each pair they found. In fact, five minutes was not long enough to solve twenty matrices; finishing the task was impossible.

At the end of the task, the students were asked to write down on a separate piece of paper how many matrices they had solved, to drop their own performance reports into a box, and to collect the appropriate payment. Since their names were not written on the matrix sheets, the students believed there was no way to trace their actual performance and they could easily cheat. In fact, the researchers had developed a way to trace actual performance and compare it with reported performance, so they would know if the students had cheated. There was no difference in the actual performance of the two groups, but the group sitting in the dimly lit room cheated more than the group who sat in the well-lit one.

You might dismiss this finding as insignificant, thinking that it is easier for students to cheat in a dim room, where they think they will not be caught because there is less chance of being seen. But this is not the case here, because the students in both rooms were sure that there was no way to trace their actual performance and that no one would know if they had cheated. It seems then that the association between darkness and immoral behaviour and between light and moral behaviour affects our actual behaviour. The study suggests that even if someone is alone in a room and absolutely anonymous, darkness still promotes more cheating. Psychologically, we are more susceptible to cheating in a dim room, or, to say it differently, we are less likely to cheat in a room full of light.

Other behaviours might also be influenced by the amount of light in the environment. The same researchers conducted an experiment in which they investigated whether the experience of darkness is related to unfair and selfish behaviour. They divided their participants into two groups: those in one group were asked to wear sunglasses, while the other group wore clear glasses. The participants were then asked to play the Dictator Game, which is often used in psychological experiments to examine fairness and morality. In this game there are two players: one is the initiator, and one is the recipient. The initiator receives a certain amount of money and decides how much of it she will give to the recipient. The recipient in turn can choose to accept or reject the money. The idea behind the Dictator Game is that the more money you give as an initiator, the less selfish you are. A 'fair share' would be half of the money. For the study, however, all the participants were given the role of initiator and got to decide how much money they'd give. They interacted via computer and could not see the other players.

Those who wore sunglasses, shading their view of the world, gave less money to the other person than those who wore clear glasses. Furthermore, those wearing sunglasses gave much less than what was fair, taking most of the money for themselves. Those with the clear glasses were fairer, giving about half of the money to the other person.

These results are definitely not trivial. But why should something as harmless as wearing sunglasses affect our moral behaviour? The participants were sitting alone in the room and interacting via computer. Wearing sunglasses simply gave them an environmental cue of darkness; they would have remained anonymous whether or not they'd worn dark glasses. Yet, seeing the world as darker degraded moral behaviour, just as the metaphors suggest. Darkness, or a darker view of the world around us, can lead to 'darker' impulses.

Does It Have to Be So Black and White?

If brightness and darkness indeed influence our judgement, behaviour and emotions, then we should give more thought to the brightness of our environment. In order to brighten up your life, think about the rooms in which you regularly spend your time: your bedroom, your office, your living room. Do you usually open the curtains or blinds? What about the kids' rooms? Research has shown that these small details can have a great influence on your quality of life.

When Norman E. Rosenthal, a South African doctor, moved to New York in the 1980s to continue his medical training, he noticed that he became less energetic in the winter. Being accustomed to sunny Johannesburg, Rosenthal suspected that the change in his mood and energy levels was related to the decreased exposure to sunlight he experienced in wintertime New York.

Around the same time, Rosenthal and his colleagues were doing research at the National Institute of Mental Health. In 1984 they noticed that people tend to experience depressive symptoms during certain seasons, year after year. Rosenthal called this now well-established phenomenon *seasonal affective disorder (SAD),* and it is known to be related to the light–dark cycles of the seasons and to affect our mental and physical processes.

Most researchers believe that SAD symptoms are caused by lack of exposure to natural light. Seasonal affective disorder occurs more often in the winter and is particularly notable in places with fewer hours of daylight, such as New England and Scandinavia. It is found less in Florida and Southern California, where people have more light hours. The most common treatment is phototherapy: exposure to artificial bright light, which mimics natural sunlight and has been shown to improve patients' moods, most likely because light affects biological and chemical processes in our bodies.

It is interesting that the influence of light is not restricted to clinical disorders. For example, a group of Canadian researchers[10] asked 48 individuals to wear a light meter on their wrist for twenty days in winter and/or summer and recorded their behaviours, moods and interactions.

Participants reported better mood and more positive interactions when they were exposed to bright light. This was true regardless of the season or the time of day. In another study, a group of researchers from Finland, where there are prolonged periods of darkness, found that workers who were exposed to bright light during their normal night shifts reported an improvement in their well-being.[11] The popular allure of a sunny tropical vacation during the dark winter months has to be due partly to the increased light, which improves mood and sociability.

After we lived in Cambridge for four years, my family and I returned to Israel, where I got my tenure-track position in the Psychology Department at Tel Aviv University. I was so thrilled to have landed the job that I didn't ask for a window office or a big laboratory, unlike today's young professors. My office, like the offices of all the other new professors, was a windowless room, completely dark unless you turned on the only light fixture, a fluorescent tube whose light was a far cry from natural daylight. Whenever I turned the key in the lock and stepped into my office, it was pitch-black. Even after I turned on the light, it seemed dark.

Those first years at my job were difficult. 'Publish or perish' is not just a saying. I had to publish my research work in high-quality international journals in order to receive tenure and the security that goes with it. I was extremely stressed, with three small children and a husband who worked as a medical doctor until late at night and was not around much to help with the kids. I went to the office every day and spent my time writing articles, instructing students, and preparing lectures. I did not feel good there for a long time and remember sitting in that office as feeling overwhelmingly negative. At the time, I attributed this negativity to the situation: always working under pressure, doing my best to earn tenure, and trying to raise my kids at the same time.

I got my tenure, and a year later I was given a nicer office, a normal room with large windows. Since the sun shines nearly all year in Israel, the office was almost always bright. Even though I knew I had this job for as long as I wanted it, I was ambitious and wanted to be promoted to associate professor and then to full professor, so I had to continue working hard and publishing in respected journals. The children were still young, my husband still did not help much, and life was still very stressful, but I definitely felt better, brighter, and much happier once I moved into my new office. Even though I had been pleased when my tenure came through, I still had negative feelings whenever I sat in that dark, windowless office – until I moved to my new, bright office.

At the time, sitting in that dark room, experiencing the difficulties of academic life, I did not believe that the office itself was an issue. That dark office had been private and quiet, a refuge where I could sit, read and write. It was a dream come true! Besides, in those early days of my career, there was nothing much I could do about the situation. I had been given that office, and I had to work there. But the dark definitely added to my gloomy emotional experience. I believe now that had I been sitting in a bright office, my life in the department would have seemed brighter. When I recall these days now, I still relive the stressful feelings I associate with the darkness of the room.

In your daily life you can take many opportunities to improve your mood. Expose yourself to sunlight by opening windows or going outside – even for just a few minutes. Even if you do like to sit in a room with the blinds drawn and only the light of a single reading lamp, the studies in this chapter clearly demonstrate that if you want things to seem more positive, you should brighten up your room. When you see that your children are in a bad mood, take them outside for some activity in the sunlight. It's a simple solution. Try to prevent your kids from sitting for hours in a semi-dark room, with only the dim light of the computer, video games, or a cell phone. Even if they say they like the dark, you now know that this darkness may unconsciously affect their mood and judgement and make them perceive their environment and the world around them negatively. If you have moody teens, ask yourself if they are getting enough light.

Even though I know about the effects of darkness from my own experience, when I am down in the dumps I still prefer to sequester myself in a semi-dark room, but whenever I resist that urge and make myself go out into the sun instead, I feel much better. When you are in a bad mood, take a walk, get outside. Then sit in a favourite café in an open space, if possible close to a body of water. I know that my spirits are soothed and my mood is improved mainly because I am looking at the sea and listening to the waves, but I now know that it is also the bright light of the sun that helps me see things in a more positive way. It will help you too.

Space, the Mental Frontier: Physical and Psychological Distance

When I talk about our position in space, I'm not talking about a grand, galactic view of the universe that requires we visit a planetarium. No doubt such a visit would be interesting, but that is not my area of expertise. Here I'm referring to our own personal space. Without our noticing it, how we occupy space – whether we sit high or low, far from or close to others, and whether we take up a lot of space or only a little – influences our judgements and behaviours in the most amazing ways.

The notion that the orientation of objects and people in space is significant is not new. Practitioners of feng shui, the ancient Chinese art of harmonious architecture and interior decoration, believe that we can improve our lives by optimally positioning people, objects and buildings in our environment. Exactly where we choose to sit in a room is considered of utmost importance in determining our success and well-being. For example, it is believed that it is better to sit with one's back to the wall, facing as much of the room as possible; and if many people occupy the room, it is best for everyone to be able to see everyone else. Although these suggestions are rooted in traditional Chinese beliefs about the universe rather than in experimental evidence, the practice of feng shui has been adopted by many Western designers and architects to good effect and to their clients' satisfaction.

The relationship of physical distance to psychological distance was suggested more than 60 years ago in a now classic study by Leon Festinger, Stanley Schachter and Kurt Back, who examined how physical proximity affects friendships.[1] Specifically, they investigated how physical closeness between the rooms in MIT dorms influenced residents' feelings about each other and found that friendship was related to physical closeness. Residents in the dorms more often categorised residents who lived close to them as friends.

The fact that we often befriend our neighbours is not really big news. All other things being equal, it makes perfect sense that the nearer two people are physically, the greater the chance they will be friends. It is simply easier to get to know each other and to interact when we live or work nearby. Although we would like to believe that we choose friends on the basis of their values and characteristics, we can admit that proximity plays a major role. Physical distance matters, and people become friends with their next-door neighbours more often than with those who live one block away. People often become long-term friends with those who slept in the bunk next to them at summer camp or in the army. The reverse is also true, as many of us experience the drifting apart of long-distance relationships and friendships.

However, the question I want to raise in this chapter is more complicated: Can physical distance activate the abstract concepts of emotional distance? Do metaphors such as *close relations, emotional distance* and *we grew apart* suggest that emotional distance is rooted in physical distance?

In an episode of *Seinfeld*, Elaine has a new boyfriend whom Jerry calls a 'close talker' – that is, a person who stands too close to others when speaking with them. Jerry hates this man's behaviour and suggests that everyone should know what a proper conversational distance is. *Seinfeld* expresses a common reaction: we don't usually like 'close talkers' who invade our personal space, and we all have an optimal distance from others that we maintain, a personal space in which we feel comfortable. This personal space has many layers or zones. The closest layer, or intimate zone, is reserved for people who are very close to us, like our partners and children. The next layer, or personal zone, is the distance we keep when talking with good friends. Then there is the social zone, or the distance we keep from people we don't know, such as salespeople or strangers who approach us to ask a question.

I was sitting in a small falafel place the other day when a stranger leaned in until his face was very close to mine to ask me how the falafel was. I was very uncomfortable, to the point of feeling threatened by his invasion of my personal space. On the other hand, if my granddaughter had done the same thing, I would have been completely comfortable.

Scientists have long believed that the discomfort we feel when our personal space is violated is an evolutionary adaptation designed to alert us when another person is close enough to do bodily harm. Recently, however, neurologists have located the part of our brain that apparently controls this response: the amygdala, which is located in the temporal lobes. Researchers at Caltech had the rare opportunity to study the role of the amygdala in governing the notion of personal space when they encountered a woman, referred to in the study as S.M., with extensive amygdala lesions.[2] The researchers put the woman through a series of tests and found that S.M.'s idea of 'too close' is far closer than that of her average peers. The Caltech scientists then conducted a series of tests on subjects whose amygdalas were not impaired and, using MRI scanning, found that normal amygdalas lit up when researchers stood too close, even when the subjects could not see the offending parties.

Another group of researchers found that people whose personal space is invaded want to assert their individuality and to separate themselves from others.[3] In one study, students were divided into two groups: those in one group sat in the front part of the room and relatively far from one another; those in the other group sat in the rear, crowded together. All participants were given a task that was unrelated to the study, after which those who sat in the rear of the room were asked to move to the front for the next experiment, ostensibly because the computers at the back of the room were not working. Participants in the crowded group from the rear of the room were asked to sit very close to their new neighbours in the front. Once everyone was re-seated, the researchers measured the participants' willingness to stand out from others by asking them to imagine that they were shopping online and to choose among four T-shirts that were identical in all aspects except for the colour of the logos printed on the shirts. Three T-shirts had a blue logo that differed somewhat in hue, and one T-shirt had a distinctive orange logo.

After choosing their T-shirts, participants were asked three questions that measured their feelings about their neighbours: Did they feel close to them, comfortable sitting with them, and similar to them? The students who had not moved but who were joined by those who came from the rear of the room felt more negatively about their neighbours now that they were crowded together than they had when they were not crowded. However, this was not true of those who had moved from the rear to the front. They did not feel that their space had been invaded since they had had to relocate, and had more positive feelings about their neighbours.

Those who stayed sitting at the front of the room chose the T-shirt with the orange logo more often when their personal space was invaded. In contrast, movers were less likely to make a unique choice when they sat close to their neighbours. These results suggest that people want to assert their individuality in a crowded place only when they feel that their space is being invaded by others. The study itself was conducted in Hong Kong, and it is related to consumer behaviour rather than to individuality in general.

Similar results were obtained in a second experiment, in which participants volunteered for an ostensible marketing study and were divided into two groups. Participants in one group could sit where they chose, while participants in the other group were told where to sit. In each group, some participants crowded close together and others did not. As in the first experiment, participants were asked to imagine that they were shopping online and were presented with four pictures, this time of coffee cups, three very similar and one different. Again, among those who were told where to sit, those in the crowded condition chose the unique cup more often than those in the uncrowded condition. The reverse was true when participants chose their seats – they wanted to sit close to others and therefore felt the need to assert their individuality not when they sat close but rather when they sat far from each other.

These results suggest that there is a difference in purchasing patterns if customers decide to enter a crowded place as opposed to entering a relatively empty space that suddenly becomes crowded. Think of going to a big sale: people who stand in line and wait for the store to open generally know they are going to shop in a very crowded place. In this case, they do not necessarily feel that their personal space is invaded and they are likely to want to buy what everybody is buying, the bargains or the new iPhones. By contrast, when someone enters an empty store and suddenly a group of people come in, all looking at the same rack, there is a good chance that the first person will go to a different store. That person feels that her space is invaded and wants to reassert her individuality.

The desire to be individual is also evident in other domains, such as expressing opinions. It would be interesting to examine what happens in the boardroom of a company, for example, if people sit very close together and feel that their personal space is invaded. The results suggest that in some cases, people might express more varied, unique opinions and perhaps even vote differently.

Our personal space is so psychologically important that even computer scientists and engineers who are building robot assistants are using psychology to improve their designs. It's important that a robot is given good manners. When we imagine robot receptionists, tour guides, office assistants and attendants that will help the elderly, we see them integrating into the human environment with respect for simple cultural practices like personal space.[4] We need our personal space, even if it is only with a robot.

Out of Sight, Out of Mind?

Over the last two decades, long-distance communication has gotten dramatically easier thanks to new technologies. The Internet, e-mail, Skype, Facebook, video conferencing and text messaging allow for immediate communication and enable conversations between people who are thousands of miles apart. Many people work from home and communicate with their co-workers, superiors, employees and customers without being in the same room or even in the same state or country. Negotiations over sales, salaries and contracts are increasingly conducted by parties who have never seen each other in person. Even friends and family members talk much less and send text messages or e-mails when they could talk to each other on the phone. We often do this in order to save time and money, but how does remote communication affect us? Does physical distance put psychological and emotional distance between us?

Communicating at a distance is usually less emotional than

communicating in person. Less hostility is manifested in e-negotiations than in face-to-face negotiations due to the absence of non-verbal cues.[5] However, since tone is so difficult to read in e-mails, statements might be interpreted as being more hostile (or less so) than they would be if communicated by phone or in person. The fact that we can now communicate so easily via e-mail and Skype with people who live and work very far away from us flattens the world, as Thomas Friedman has written, bridging the distance and giving us the sense that physical separation is not so important. Nonetheless, there is still a big difference between remote and face-to-face communication, and distance still matters.

I was a member of the executive board of Tel Aviv University for several years, one of three professors who represented the university senate, along with the president and the provost of the university. The other members of the executive board were people outside the university and included high-tech entrepreneurs, businesspeople, industrialists, lawyers, bankers and journalists – all very successful and well known in their fields. Board meetings could be somewhat intimidating, but I felt I could express my opinions freely, even if some of the people did not agree with me. When I sat physically close to these people, I felt emotionally closer to them and therefore less intimidated.

When I relocated for a few months to San Diego and New York while on sabbatical leave, I still regularly attended the board meetings, but via telephone. I was very attentive and heard everything that was said, but it felt completely different from being in the same room. I felt psychologically distant. Videoconferencing would probably have been better, but I believe that there is no substitute for a good old-fashioned meeting in which everyone is in the same room.

I also know this from experience with my family. My four granddaughters live thousands of miles away from me, in California. Naturally I miss them a lot and use every opportunity I have to talk to them, preferably via Skype, with which I can not only hear them but also see them. Skype is better than talking on the phone, because with Skype I can detect more non-verbal cues. Still, it is not the same as being with my granddaughters in the same room. I feel the physical distance. I can't touch them, and I can't really get close to them.

In the 2009 movie *Up in the Air,* based on the novel by Walter Kirn, the protagonist, Ryan Bingham, portrayed by George Clooney, flies all over the United States for his job, which is to fire people employed at various companies face-to-face. A newly hired young woman colleague proposes that they fire people via videoconference rather than travelling to meet them, pointing out that communicating via video would be much more efficient and cost-effective. But Ryan believes the firing should be done in person. This disagreement represents a larger issue that we face in the modern world. Does it matter if we talk face-to-face, or is it preferable to depersonalise communication and do everything via conference calls, e-mails, and so forth? Does physical distance still matter in a world of digital communication?

More and more people interact virtually, shop and listen to lectures online, and talk via the Internet and Facebook. But while our social life has a significant online component, many of our most important social relationships occur in real physical space. We live in the same house with our family and interact with partners, children, parents and siblings; go to work, attend lectures, meet friends at restaurants, attend plays and concerts, and pick up our children from school. We're also supposed to break off relationships in person, whether that's firing someone or ending an intimate relationship. It is still considered rude to do this via text message or e-mail – or even by mail or phone. In one episode of the popular television series *Sex and the City*, Carrie Bradshaw wakes up to find that her boyfriend Berger has broken up with her by leaving a Post-it note stuck to her laptop. Carrie and her friends are furious. There is a clear consensus among them that the only decent way to end a relationship is face-to-face.

The question I want to raise here is whether metaphors that use physical distance to describe psychological distance are grounded in our physical experiences.

Physical and Emotional Distance

What characterises an emotionally distant person? When I posed this question to my students, they described someone whose emotions are not easily affected by events occurring around him or her – whether happy, frightening, or distressing. People who are emotionally distant cry less at movies; they don't react emotionally to tragic or exciting events around them or reported in the news; they are less involved in the lives of other people. They tend to show less empathy and compassion.

In order to examine whether physical distance evokes feelings of emotional and psychological distance, researchers asked participants to mark two points on a Cartesian plane.[6] Here is what the plane looked like:

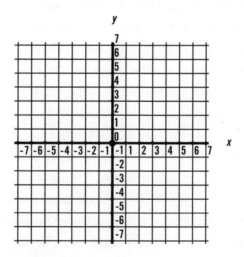

The researchers divided the participants into two groups. One group was asked to mark two relatively close points; the aim was to induce in this group an experience of physical closeness. The other group was asked to mark two points that were relatively far apart; in this case the aim was to induce an experience of physical distance. The only difference between these two groups was marking relatively close or distant points.

Participants were then asked to read a passage from *Good in Bed*, a popular novel by Jennifer Weiner, in which the heroine discovers a magazine article that her ex-boyfriend has written entitled 'Loving a Larger Woman'. The article turns out to be about her and understandably provokes a range of emotions in her. Participants were asked whether they enjoyed the excerpt, whether they found it entertaining, and whether they would like to continue reading the book. The researchers expected that the plotting of physical distance on the graph would influence how emotionally distant the participants felt. The results confirmed their predictions: those who were asked to mark two points relatively far from each other liked the embarrassing passage and found it more enjoyable than those who were asked to locate two close points, who found it uncomfortable and embarrassing.

This amazing influence of physical distance on psychological distance was demonstrated again, this time using a violent passage. Researchers asked participants to read about two brothers injured in a car accident in which one brother is so badly hurt that he begs the other to kill him. This time, instead of asking the participants whether they liked the text (in the hope that no one enjoyed such a terrible story), the researchers asked them to rate their emotions, giving them a list of positive and negative emotions and mood descriptors, such as *enthusiastic, upset, distressed* and *excited*. Those who had marked close points reported significantly more negative emotions than those who had marked far points. Remember, all they had done before reading was to mark two points.

These two studies demonstrate clearly that there is an association between spatial cues and our emotions, and that exposure to certain physical concepts triggers the cues for the related concept in our minds, affecting our outlook and emotions.

The Closer the Better? It Depends ...

These results enable us to see ways of using our environment to affect others and ourselves. I am sure that at some point in your life, you have needed to have a serious conversation with your partner, children, parents, friends, colleagues, or boss. In the future, spend a couple of seconds before beginning an important conversation by positioning yourself at a distance that best suits the message you are about to deliver. Consider how you should sit next to a date or across from a job interviewer. Sometimes you want the people with whom you are negotiating to be logical rather than emotional, and sometimes you want them to be influenced by their emotions. It all comes down to the type of conversation you are having.

For example, if you talk with your boss about a raise, is it better if the boss is emotionally close or distant? The answer might depend on the reasons you use for asking for the raise. If you bring to the conversation your personal difficulties and how much you need the money, then it might be better that the boss is prompted to feel emotionally close. That way, she will better understand your needs and perhaps show more empathy, increasing your chance of getting the raise. By contrast, if you tell the boss that another company has offered you a higher salary and you would like her to match or exceed it, then it might be better that the boss is not emotionally close, since you want her to make a logical decision and not be influenced by emotions such as anger or jealousy. In this case it might be better to sit a bit farther than usual from the boss.

Imagine you want to have an important talk with your spouse

and bring to her attention that she is not spending enough time with you. In this case, you want your partner to be emotionally close to you. You want empathy. You want your partner to understand how difficult it is for you that she is rarely there. This conversation will be much more effective if you sit close to each other. On the other hand, if you want to tell your boss that you're quitting your job, you would probably prefer him to be emotionally distant and might take a seat that puts more space than usual between you. Similarly, if you want to tell your parents that you intend to marry someone for whom they don't care much, or that you are going to major in a subject of which they don't approve ('Philosophy? What's wrong with business administration?'), do not sit too close to them. By increasing the physical distance, you increase the emotional and psychological distance. Your parents may still be upset, but by giving them some space you will make it easier for them and you to look at things more objectively.

If you are going to have one of these meaningful conversations in a restaurant, decide beforehand whether you want the other party to be psychologically distant or close, and choose a table accordingly. For some conversations you might be better off picking a restaurant with relatively large tables, where you'll have a bigger expanse of table between you. For other conversations, you may get better results by sitting at a small, intimate table or even side by side. If you are going on a first date, decide beforehand whether you want the other person to feel emotionally close or distant, then pick a restaurant accordingly. At home, think about how to foster more closeness in your family. Is your dinner table long, keeping distance between family members, or do you crowd together around a table, elbows touching?

The psychological distance between couples is demonstrated dramatically in many movies, especially the classics, where husband and wife are at opposite ends of a formal, very long table. This physical distance symbolises their emotional distance. Even if a dinner table is not large, when family members are seated far apart in a relatively formal arrangement, it reflects a lack of intimacy in the home. This is portrayed very effectively in the now iconic dinner table scene in *American Beauty.*

Architects who design work spaces and public facilities can use these findings to develop a better understanding of the psychological influence of interpersonal distance. If proximity is indeed related to emotional closeness, then there should be places where co-workers can actually stand close to one another and talk and gather together comfortably to brainstorm. A workplace with cubicles in which each employee has a personal space lends itself to individual effort, but a larger room where several people are sitting next to one another can promote group effort. It all depends on your intention for the space.

You can use this same knowledge when remodelling your home or buying furniture. Think carefully about where you place the chairs and the sofas, and how to decorate your office. If you have a very long table at home that can easily seat twelve but you have only four people over for dinner, consider whether you want each one to sit on one side of the table, or whether to use only half of the table so that all the diners are seated closer together. This will surely influence the atmosphere and the intimacy of the conversation. There is no right answer in any of these decisions. It depends on who the guests are and whether you want them to feel emotionally close or more distant. The studies cited here showed that just marking close or distant points on a Cartesian graph influenced psychological distance. It is possible then that not only the distance between people, but even the distance between the plates and the serving dishes on the table influences our psychological states.

Consider these findings also when you are deciding where to live. I grew up in an apartment house that belonged to my grandparents, who lived in a different apartment in the same building, as did two of my father's brothers. I remember it as a negative experience rife with tension, which I believe could have been avoided were we not so physically close. By that, I do not mean to say that physical closeness is bad. I mean to say, rather, that it is related to emotional closeness that can be good or bad, depending on the people involved and on the circumstances. In our case, emotional distance would have been much better.

Many couples maintain long-distance relationships and live quite far from one another. Studies of these kinds of relationships indicate that physical distance can have both a detrimental and a beneficial effect. While some couples find the distance stressful, others report feeling that 'absence makes the heart grow fonder' and that while in close proximity, they miss having more personal space.[7]

More studies are needed to investigate other areas in which physical distance influences psychological distance, and whether physical distance has greater influence on some people than on others. The results of the studies cited in this chapter nevertheless strongly suggest that just experiencing cues of physical distance not necessarily related directly to us can be enough to evoke an emotional reaction. Emotional distance is related to physical distance.

High and Mighty:
Vertical Position, Size and Power

In the previous chapter we talked about physical distance and learned that this aspect of our location in space influences emotional distance. In this chapter I will talk about two additional dimensions of space – vertical positioning and size – and how they influence our thoughts, feelings, judgements, decisions and behaviours. As we shall see, all the evidence indicates that we intuitively link height and size to power. Occasionally, but not always, vertical positioning and size overlap; for instance, a tall person may be perceived not only as being high up on the vertical scale but also as being large.

Let's Take It from the Top: Vertical Positioning and Power

An amusing scene in Charlie Chaplin's film *The Great Dictator* nicely demonstrates the perceived advantage of being physically higher than others. In the scene, the titular dictator, Adenoid Hynkel, is preparing to meet with his ally, fellow dictator Benzino Napaloni. Just before the meeting, Hynkel's adviser briefs him on all the psychological tactics he will employ to make Napaloni feel inferior: first, he will enter the room at the far opposite door, forcing Napaloni to make a humiliating walk across the floor to Hynkel, and on arrival Napaloni will be seated in a lower position, ensuring that he will always be looking up at the great dictator. (Incidentally, though *The Great Dictator* is obviously an exaggerated satire, the architect Albert Speer reported that long, exhausting corridors were a prominent, intentional feature of Hitler's plans for the postwar chancellery.) The plan backfires when Napaloni enters the room directly behind Hynkel's chair, surprising him, and refuses to sit in the 'baby stool' provided for him. Napaloni then stands over the seated Hynkel and, at one point, sits on the comically large desk with his back turned to him. After the meeting, the two men go for a shave and find themselves competing once again for a higher position, each trying to outdo the other in elevating the hydraulic chairs. Hynkel never gains the high ground.

In 2010, following criticism of Israel by Turkish prime minister Tayyip Erdoğan and a negative portrayal of Israelis on a popular Turkish television drama, Israeli deputy foreign minister Danny Ayalon summoned the Turkish ambassador to a meeting. He seated Ambassador Çelikkol on a sofa that was lower, by several feet, than his own chair. Asking the ambassador to sit in a lower position, looking up at the unsmiling faces of his Israeli counterparts, was considered an egregious public humiliation, which anyone who saw the photos intuitively understood. Following this incident, which was met with harsh criticism in Israel and Turkey, the slighted Turkish ambassador was recalled to Ankara; his recall very nearly triggered a breakdown in diplomatic relations between Israel and Turkey.

Politics (both real and satirical) aside, height and vertical positioning constitute critical social symbols, for we associate vertical positioning with power, equating being high above others with being powerful and being low with powerlessness.

The association between power and vertical positioning is embedded deeply within us and expressed in many colourful metaphors: *He looks up to his brother; she thinks very highly of herself; he's higher in the pecking order at work; she climbed the corporate ladder; he's working under her on a very important project; take him down a few pegs.*

According to embodied cognition theory, we don't just speak metaphorically; we also think metaphorically. And we actually represent the concept of power visually in our minds. This representation was examined by a group of researchers. They have shown that whenever we are asked to draw the relationship between powerful and powerless groups, we choose to draw them on a vertical line, with the powerful group always at the top and the powerless group invariably at the bottom.[1]

In a second experiment, the researchers examined whether we automatically and unconsciously associate power with vertical positioning. They presented participants with pairs of words on a computer screen that represented two parties in a power-imbalanced relationship, such as employer and employee, army officer and private, master and servant, and judge and defendant. One party always represented the powerful group and the other a less powerful group. The pairings were presented vertically, with one word appearing at the top of the screen and the other at the bottom. Then participants were asked to indicate as fast as possible, by pressing a key, which in each pair was powerful and which powerless. The results were in line with the Stroop effect that we've read about in previous chapters: it took longer for participants to identify the powerful items when they were at the bottom of the screen. And it took longer to identify the powerless parties when they were positioned at the top of the screen.

For example, it was easier to identify the word *employee* as a powerless word when it was presented at the bottom of the screen. Participants reacted faster when the powerful or powerless words were in their intuitively correct vertical positions.

Another experiment found that when test subjects viewed words that represented powerful groups, the upward dimension was automatically and unconsciously activated and their attention shifted to the top of the screen.[2] When they saw words representing powerless groups, their attention shifted to the bottom of the screen.

In a further study, participants were presented with images of animals on a computer screen.[3] Each picture appeared for a very short time (800 milliseconds, less than a second). Participants were asked to indicate on a scale of 1 to 9 the degree of respect they would have for each animal if they encountered it in the wild. Some of the pictures were of traditionally powerful animals, such as lions, tigers, wolves and polar bears, while some were of harmless animals, such as sheep, squirrels and rabbits. Participants indicated more respect for the so-called powerful animals when they appeared on the top of the screen than when they appeared on the bottom. There was no such effect for powerless animals.

These results demonstrate that we perceive power as embodied in a vertical position. Without our awareness, vertical positioning influences what we characterise as powerful. We are apt to perceive a taller person or a person who sits on a higher chair as more powerful.

Bottom Lines and Corporate Ladders: Position in Business

Another group of researchers looked into the connection between position and status in business.[4] Subjects were shown a chart that represented the organisational structure of a fictitious company. There were two levels in the organisation chart. At the lower level were five boxes connected by a horizontal line; the upper level consisted of a single box connected by a vertical line to the box in the middle of the lower level. The upper box represented the manager and included a small photo, depicting a middle-aged man in a suit.

Participants were divided into two groups, the only difference between the groups being the length of the vertical line connecting the manager to the lower level on the charts they were shown. One group received a chart in which the vertical line was 2cm long. The other group received the same chart but with a vertical line 7cm in length. Participants were then asked to evaluate the manager on five characteristics, including dominance, status, and the control he exercised in the company, all signifiers of power. They were also asked to evaluate the manager's charisma, i.e. how enthusiastic and inspiring he was, a characteristic not necessarily related to authority.

The researchers found that participants who were given the chart with the longer vertical line evaluated the manager as being more powerful than those who were given the chart with the shorter line. In contrast, the length of the vertical line did not influence the perceived charisma of the manager.

The researchers also examined the phenomenon in reverse. Subjects were given profiles of managers or leaders who were described as being either powerful or powerless. They were then given an organisational chart and asked to place the square of the manager on the chart. The results demonstrated that the positioning of the square was directly influenced by the information about the managers' or leaders' power. Those who read a description of a powerful manager placed the manager's square higher than those who read a description of an unpowerful manager. Similar results were found when participants were given photographs rather than squares and asked to place them on the chart. The more powerful the leader was, the greater the distance they left between leaders and the lower level on the chart.

These results have important implications for presentations of companies and organisations. A flow chart often employs symbols to make it easier to understand the potentially complicated structure of an organisation. We all know that when we view or present an organisational chart, those who are more powerful are represented above those who are less powerful. However, these findings demonstrate that the length of the line between the levels is also of great significance. If you want to stress the importance of a certain unit or a certain role in the organisation when making a presentation to potential investors, buyers, or donors, make the line between that unit and the level below it longer.

The association between vertical positioning and power is so strong that even the mere length of a line influences our perception of how much power someone holds. We lift and float powerful ideas and images to the 'top' of our mind's eye. To use this association in advertising, for example, display the name of a company or the powerful attribute of the company in a high position on a billboard, screen, or page.

We now turn to an obvious measurement in the dimension of vertical positioning, height.

The Size of Success: Subjectivity of Height

In a clever study, Canadian researchers compared the estimated heights of politicians before and after elections.[5] They found that Brian Mulroney, the businessman from Montreal whose party won the Canadian federal elections in 1988, was judged as taller after the elections. The reverse was true for those who lost that election; they were estimated to be shorter after losing than before running for office. These results suggest that the association between power and height goes both ways. Not only do we perceive taller people as being more powerful, but we also perceive powerful people as taller than they actually are. In other words, once people get placed in a position of power or authority, they 'grow' in stature.

My paternal grandparents' family was, for me, the epitome of a patriarchal clan. My grandfather was undoubtedly the dominant figure in the home, and everybody – his wife, his children, and we, his grandchildren – had great respect for him and even feared him a little. Exceedingly intelligent, wealthy and knowledgeable, he was our prime source of reliable information in my pre-Internet youth. When we'd gather at my grandparents' house for Friday dinners and holidays, my grandfather presided like a king, always sitting at the head of the table while my grandmother and other members of the family served him. When he spoke, no one interrupted him. Nobody ever argued with him. If we children made any noise, the word *quiet* from his lips would instantly silence us.

I had always thought of my grandfather as tall. In my mind, he was taller than most people around him. It was only after he died, while looking at pictures taken throughout his life, that I realised my memories of his stature were wrong. In reality, he was shorter than both of his sons and, generally speaking, on the shorter side of average. The pictures in my hands showed him to be average in height at best, but even then I checked with my mother to verify what my eyes were seeing. Even after learning that the grandfather I had always thought of as being tall was actually short, I still see him in my memory as towering over the rest of the family.

There is ample evidence that a strong relationship exists between height and professional success and leadership.[6] Tall people receive higher salaries on average and tend to be disproportionately represented in high-status jobs, even when the data account for the level of education and the physical strength required for the job. There are more tall CEOs and managers than not, and most American presidents were taller than average (though James Madison stood at a

slight five feet four). Several studies have even found a positive correlation between height and subjective well-being.[7]

There may be many reasons why taller individuals tend to be more
successful. Several researchers have suggested that adolescents who are
taller than average are more popular and consequently have more opportunities to acquire social skills, and that they have higher self-esteem – all
of which help them later in life.[8] One of the main reasons for this phenomenon is that we associate height with power. Therefore, other things
being more or less equal, the taller person is often perceived as more powerful and consequently attributed more authority and dominance. Taller
individuals are more frequently awarded good jobs and higher salaries,
which reinforce the association between power and stature.

Pick On Someone Your Own Size

Even though we perceive powerful people as taller than average, our
impression of their height depends also on how powerful *we* feel in
comparison. Our subjective impression of height (for both ourselves
and those we observe) depends on a power struggle within our minds.

To test this phenomenon, researchers divided participants into two
groups and then manipulated how powerful or powerless they felt.[9]
Those in one group were asked to write about a past experience where
they had power over someone else; those in the other group were
asked to write about an experience in which they felt at the mercy
of others. The researchers then presented the groups with a picture
of a person and asked them to estimate that person's height. Those
who had recalled a powerful experience tended to underestimate the
height of the person in the picture, and those who had recalled a powerless experience tended to overestimate the person's height. In other
words, for those who felt powerful, the person in the picture seemed
shorter, and vice versa.

In the second experiment, the researchers directly manipulated the experience of power. They invited the participants to the laboratory in pairs and asked them to play the Dictator Game (mentioned in chapter 6), in which there are two roles: the officer (or dictator) and the receiver. The officer is given ten dollars and exerts sole discretion over how the money is to be divided between himself or herself and the receiver. The officer therefore has full control over the situation. The receiver is completely powerless. Participants were randomly assigned to these roles.

Following the game, participants were asked to estimate their partners' weight and height. Just as in the first study, those who were assigned the role of the dictator and therefore felt powerful underestimated the weight and the height of their partners. In contrast, those who had the misfortune to be the lowly receivers, and therefore felt powerless, saw their respective dictators as larger and taller than they really were.

Similar studies have shown that perceived power affects how we think of our own height as well. In two experiments, researchers manipulated how powerful participants felt, either by asking them to recall a powerful or powerless event or by placing them in a business simulation in which they were assigned either a powerful role (the manager) or a powerless role (an employee).[10] Participants were then given a pole that was specifically adjusted to be 50cm longer than each participant's height. The participant was then asked to indicate his or her own height on that pole. Those in the high-power group estimated themselves as taller than those in the low-power group.

The more powerful we feel, the taller we perceive ourselves and the shorter we perceive others to be. Once again, it's clear that physical perception, even of an objective attribute such as height, is often influenced by our emotional and mental states.

No doubt you've seen a man in an enormous four-by-four sitting high above traffic and wondered what he might be compensating for. Granted, this pop psychological insight is more often than not invoked in jest, and many would argue for the security benefits of large vehicles. Still, there is simply no denying the association between power and stature.

The Framing of Power: Photography and the Media

Because we automatically associate vertical position with power, camera angles in pictures can affect our judgements of the people photographed. A group of researchers investigated whether media exploit this association, examining whether photos of powerful individuals and photos of less powerful persons are taken from different angles.[11] We don't need to be photographers to know that there are many angles from which one can take a picture: from a low angle, from a high angle, or straight on. When the picture is taken from below, the viewer looks up at the person in the photo.

The researchers took pictures from *The Time 100: The People Who Shaped Our World* (2006) and *The Time 100: The Most Important People of the Century* (2006), assuming that the people on these lists are powerful people. They presented the pictures of these individuals to professional photographers who were unaware of the purpose of the study and asked them to estimate the angle from which each picture was taken. The professional photographers indicated that on average the pictures were taken from below. These results suggest that the photographers and the magazine editors choose to depict powerful individuals from below to make them look more powerful.

The researchers further investigated this question by comparing photos of people from *Time* magazine with photos of the same people in Wikipedia or on their personal Facebook pages (in which what matters is social relations and not necessarily power). They found that pictures of the same people were presented from different angles depending on the context. Since the *Time* list of the most influential people has a more powerful connotation than Wikipedia and Facebook, more pictures portraying the individuals from below were presented in the former than in the latter. The more you want to present the subject as powerful (be it consciously or subconsciously), the more you change the angle of the photo.

To compare these photographs with photos of powerless individuals, the researchers chose pictures from the 2007 World Press Photo contest gallery, which includes a range of notable press photographs. They asked three analysts (who were not photographers) to evaluate whether the photos depicted powerful or powerless situations, and then asked professional photographers to evaluate the angle from which each picture was taken. The pictures that represented powerful people or situations were more often taken from below, and those of powerless people or of situations such as war or poverty were more often shot from above.

The researchers also conducted a laboratory study in which they asked students to find a suitable picture for a students' association booklet. There were two conditions in the experiment. Students were asked to choose a picture for a new CEO of the students' association, and to find a photo for an assistant to help the association's secretary. In other words, one was a powerful position and the other a powerless position. Students then were asked to choose from three different pictures of the same person, which had been taken from above, from below, and from the front. The students more frequently chose a picture that was shot from below for the powerful position than for the powerless one.

Capturing Moments of Power

These results clearly demonstrate that the angle of a photograph matters. Now you know that the media may use this subconscious connection to evoke certain emotional reactions. When journalists want to present a powerful situation or a powerful person, they are likely to use low-angle pictures to manipulate perception. Next time you see a photograph of a leader, politician, or CEO in a newspaper or on the Internet, remember that the author or publisher might be using the picture to influence your judgement of that person. Think about the angle of the picture as well as the agenda of the news source before making any judgements about the story being illustrated.

The real power of understanding this phenomenon relates to managing photos of yourself! Keep this information in mind whenever you post or send your own photos for interviews, job applications, dating websites, or Facebook. Think of how you'd like to be perceived and use the right photograph with the appropriate angle.

Getting to the Bottom of Vertical Positioning and Power

In the anthropological sense, numerous acts of dominance or supplication are related to vertical positioning. Many animals – dogs, for example – establish dominance by positioning themselves higher than their rivals and pinning them to the ground.

In humans, the act of kneeling before someone is a universal sign of supplication. In a memorable scene from the classic movie *The King and I,* the king of Siam informs Anna, a governess, that in his kingdom, no person is permitted to hold his head higher than that of the king. Then, upon sitting down, he commands Anna, who is standing, to get on the floor in order to bring her head down to his level. Whether we are commoners or kings, we intuitively understand that power and height are connected. We have evolved to know that a higher position is a superior position; we can attack from or defend high ground or a high position with gravity as our ally.

As children, we are diminutive, small and low to the ground;

childhood is our most powerless time of life. From the day we are born, we look up at the adults who bend over us. Whenever a tiny, adorable, defenceless infant experiences hunger, pain, or even the smallest discomfort, he or she cries and a taller, bigger person comes. Helpless babies learn that they are totally dependent on taller, bigger people who feed, change, or comfort them, and come to their rescue when they feel uncomfortable. Toddlers, too, who are able to talk and walk, remain mostly dependent on their parents and caretakers for sustenance, guidance and amusement. Grown-ups tell them what and when to eat, where to go, and when to go to sleep. They play with them and read them stories. Not only do they extend care but they constitute total authority and occasionally punish the children. Grown-ups are the power figures.

At school, more authority figures appear in the form of teachers. Taller children and older siblings dominate younger or shorter children and in some cases even use force to get what they want. Tall teenage boys often achieve more success in sports and with girls. It is not surprising, then, that we associate height and size with power from an early age.

Even adults may feel more threatened by taller, bigger persons than by smaller ones. Taller adults, too, are more successful in many professional sports. Leaders, teachers, the clergy, professors and managers usually speak while standing on a podium in order to appear taller than they are. Gold medallists in the Olympic Games always stand on a podium that is higher than those on which the silver and bronze medallists stand. Management offices are often located on the top floor of a building. I'm sure the view is a draw, but the association exists between being high and being powerful, and managers can get a better view because they are powerful.

In established tradition from ancient civilisations to this very day, leaders build enormous monuments in extravagant displays of power and resources. The Egyptian pharaohs commissioned the pyramids ostensibly as their tombs, but the structures' towering, glimmering presence sent a message to outsiders that the pharaohs had wealth, power, and a vast army of labourers at their disposal. Across the centuries and continents, the Maya, Aztec, Inca, Chinese, Indians and Khmer all constructed huge, elaborate palaces and temples as tributes to their kings and deities and as unmistakable evidence of their authority.

Beginning in the late 1940s, Joseph Stalin ordered the construction of a number of skyscrapers in the Russian capital, Moscow, to be built in a style that drew on Gothic and Russian Baroque architecture, a style later named Stalinist. Known as Stalin's Seven Sisters, this network of residential, commercial and administrative buildings stood as oppressive symbols of Stalin's harsh dictatorship, and was clearly intended to demonstrate to his Western rivals that the dictator was fully equipped to compete with the United States. What better way to demonstrate his vast resources and technological savvy than with not one but seven skyscrapers?

The race to build the highest structure continues today. No level of modern sophistication – not smart technology, genetic engineering, or global connectivity – can tame or mask that primordial urge to ascend the highest hill, beat your chest, and proclaim that you are the highest of the high. Today, various cities and countries jostle to claim the world's tallest building, a commanding symbol of economic and national vitality. As of this writing (2013), three of the world's tallest structures have been built in the past three years alone: One World Trade Center in New York (541m); the Makkah Royal Clock Tower Hotel in Mecca, Saudi Arabia (601m); and the dizzyingly high Burj Khalifa tower in Dubai, United Arab Emirates (828m). China has announced plans to build a mammoth building called Sky City, which will exceed the height of Burj Khalifa by 10m. Even luxury condo projects advertise their impressive heights, thus adding to their lustre. A condo project in New York, 432 Park, once completed, will attain a height of 426m and thus become an iconic part of the city's skyline.

Power, Height and Physical Attraction: Tall, Dark and Handsome

What defines people like managers and presidents of big companies and high-ranking politicians and military people as powerful is the role or position they hold. Profession and status can change, but race and sex, which are more stable, are also connected with power. Evolutionary psychologists claim that since men were hunter-gatherers and women were childbearers, women needed powerful men to protect them and higher-status men to provide them with more resources, and men needed submissive young women who would deliver children and stay home to look after them.

Although times have changed and in many households both men and women work and share household responsibilities, the vestiges of our roots remain. A greater number of women still find powerful men attractive, while men are intimidated by women who are more powerful than themselves or hold higher status. It is still more common for the man to be the main provider and for the woman to care for the children. I'm aware this all sounds clichéd, and I assert these thoughts and findings grudgingly, because I happen to be a woman of science and a feminist. However, these facts are reflections of the world we live in. Let us, then, delve into the domain of physical attraction.

Two researchers wanted to examine if the association between vertical positioning and power also applies to physical attraction.[12] Since women prefer powerful men and find them more attractive, a man who is presented at the top of the computer screen should be perceived as more powerful, and thus more attractive. In contrast, if men actually prefer less powerful women, then a woman presented at the bottom of the screen will be perceived as less powerful but more attractive.

The particularly interesting aspect of the study was that the researchers did not give information about the power of the men and women; they simply manipulated their vertical positioning. They presented photos of men and women on a computer screen, to male and female students and asked them to rate the attractiveness of each photo. The photos were presented either at the top or at the bottom of the screen. The results clearly demonstrated that women found men more attractive when their photos were at the top of the screen while men rated women as more attractive when their photos were at the bottom.

In another study, researchers analysed photos of men and women on a website and compared the angles from which photos were taken.[13] They found that photos of men were more often taken from below and photos of women were more often taken from above. As we saw earlier, photos taken from below are perceived as depicting more powerful people than photos that are taken from above.

These results suggest that women and men are still portrayed in line with the stereotypes that men are powerful and dominant, while women are relatively powerless and submissive. Taken together, these studies suggest that although gender roles are undeniably evolving, men – whether or not they are aware of it – often prefer less powerful women and find them more attractive, whereas the inverse is true of female preferences for men.

Things Are Looking Up on Cloud Nine: Positivity, Negativity and the Abode of God

Vertical positioning is also related to positivity and negativity. Up is good, and down is bad. *Feeling down* is negative, while *feeling up* or *high,* or *in seventh heaven,* is positive. If a product is good, we describe it as being of *high quality*. When things are going well they *are looking up*, but when things are at their worst we might say they have *hit rock bottom*.

Using the Stroop method (described in detail in chapter 6), researchers investigated whether the association between positivity and vertical positioning is automatic.[14] Participants identified words as positive more easily when they appeared at the top of the screen. Similarly, it was easier for them to identify words as negative when they appeared at the bottom of the screen. These results suggest that the abstract concepts of positivity and negativity are represented in our minds in perceptual dimensions along a vertical axis. We automatically and unconsciously associate vertical positioning not only with power but also with positivity and negativity: up is good and down is bad.

God and the Devil, two abstract concepts that symbolise good and evil, are also related to up and down. Hell and the Devil reside beneath us, while God is invariably thought of as being 'up' in heaven and considered 'the man upstairs'. Indeed, studies have found that people automatically associate God with up and the Devil with down.

Researchers found that screen position strongly influenced subjects' ability to identify God-related and Devil-related words.[15] God-related words were identified faster when they were presented at the top of the screen, while Devil-related words were identified faster when they were presented at the bottom of the screen.

Moreover, the researchers found that this association between divinity and vertical positioning influences the way we judge others. Participants were presented with photos of various strangers that appeared at either the top or the bottom of the screen. They tended to judge people whose photos were presented at the top of the computer screen as believing in God more than strangers whose photos were presented at the bottom of the screen.

These findings suggest that the representation of divine concepts is related to perceptual and bodily experiences. Not only do many people look up when they invoke divine help or pray to God but they automatically associate positive and negative divine concepts with having an elevated and low position, respectively.

Power and Size – What's the Big Idea?

With size typically comes power. Large animals, large machines, large bodies of water – all are naturally associated with power, force and momentum. But why do we associate size with social power? Holding a high-status position that controls and evaluates others is not the same as winning a fistfight. From an evolutionary perspective, size relates to power, and large size is often a physical conduit for power. We look up to other creatures who are larger than we are. Evolutionarily, associating size with power conferred the ability to survive.

In the animal kingdom (of which we are a part), size is without a doubt an important cue in the non-verbal expression of dominance. Animals demonstrate power and dominance by taking up a lot of space and expanding and spreading their limbs. The puffer fish pumps water into its stomach and triples its size to defend itself against predators.[16] When frogs see a predator, or even when they have already been seized by one, they will fill their lungs with air and puff up to enlarge their body size.[17] The hognose snake spreads its neck to make itself appear more imposing.[18] When the jay defends its nest, it positions itself in a manner that greatly enlarges its body: its feathers stand erect, its wings are slightly spread (or fully spread in more threatening situations), the tail may be slightly spread too, and the bill is open.[19] Cats arch their backs and their fur stands on end (piloerection) when they see a potential attacker.

Chimpanzees who wish to convey their dominance raise their

arms, push out their chests, stand up so as to look bigger, sway their limbs, and often jump up and down. In so doing, the chimpanzee uses the space around him to appear bigger than he really is and, consequently, more dominant and powerful. Submissive chimpanzees lower their bodies when they encounter a dominant one, constrict themselves, take up less space, and make themselves appear smaller and non-threatening so they do not provoke an attack.[20]

A group of researchers examined whether the association between power and size is automatic by using the Stroop effect.[21] Participants were presented with powerful or powerless words, written in either large (26-point) or small (twelve-point) type. They were asked to indicate as rapidly as possible whether the word was powerful or powerless. Participants responded faster and were more accurate in identifying powerful words written in big type as well as identifying powerless words written in small type. In other words, it was easier for them to identify the words when powerful words were big and powerless words were small. These findings suggest that we automatically associate size with power and that a larger item automatically activates cues of power.

Wake Up and Smell the (Large) Coffee

Small, medium, large; short, tall and jumbo – we are constantly confronted with the task of choosing the 'correct' size for our food, clothing and other daily items. Could the sizes we select reflect how powerful we feel? Could it be that when we feel less powerful, we are more likely to choose a large coffee or smoothie to make ourselves feel better? Does seeing someone else order a large or small beverage influence how powerful we perceive that person to be?

To examine these interesting questions, a group of consumer researchers conducted several experiments.[22] In one experiment, the researchers asked participants to read several scenarios and to answer some questions about characters in them. The scenarios were always about a person who enters a smoothie shop, a pizza place, or a coffee shop and has to make a choice between three sizes: small, medium, or large. Participants were asked to judge the person in the story on various criteria: two related to status (has 'high status' and respect) and others, such as honesty and attractiveness, not directly related to status. The results showed that the people who chose the largest sizes of each of the products were judged as having higher status than those who chose the medium or small sizes. Those who chose the smallest sizes were seen as having the lowest status. The product sizes had no apparent effect on other assessments; sizes affected only the status judgements.

These findings indicate that when we see a person with a big cup of coffee, we tend to attribute more power to that person. Furthermore, when other people see us holding a big cup of coffee, they might attribute more power to us. It seems that when we want to project power, it is worth choosing the large cup of coffee, even if we drink only half of it. On the flip side, if we want to appear unassuming or are worried that we seem intimidating, stepping down the size of our purchases can send the right message.

In a second experiment, the researchers wanted to examine if our size choices are influenced by how powerful we feel. They divided 142 students into three groups and manipulated how powerful they felt by asking participants in the high-power group to recall an incident in which they wielded power over another person or persons or were in a situation in which they evaluated other people. In the low-power group, participants were asked to recall an instance in which someone else had power over them, such as evaluating them or controlling their ability to get what they wanted. Participants in the control group were asked to recall their last visit to the grocery store, a totally neutral event.

The students were then asked to participate in an ostensibly unrelated marketing study and were presented with three images of smoothies and asked which one they would choose if the smoothies were sold at the university student centre. The three photos differed in size and were labelled as small, medium and large. Participants who were in the low-power group more often chose the larger smoothies as compared with the high-power participants or with those who recalled going to the grocery store. In other words, those who felt powerless and wanted a higher status were more likely to choose a bigger size. Keep that in mind the next time you go to your local coffee shop and are deciding which size coffee you want to order: ask yourself if the size you buy has anything to do with the way you feel or want to be perceived.

The researchers wanted to make sure that it was the size of the product that was the determining factor rather than its price; after all, a large smoothie costs more than a small smoothie. In order to neutralise this variable, they designed a creative experiment. They set up tables in the lobbies of three residential buildings of the university with large banners that advertised a fictitious new bagel chain in the area. All three banners invited students to treat themselves to free bagels, but the banners differed in their content. The message on one banner said that we all feel powerless in the morning. The banner in the second lobby said that we all feel powerful in the morning, while the banner in the third lobby bore a neutral message, simply stating that it was morning.

The researcher in each lobby acted as a company representative and invited the residents to taste the bagels. There were two plates on the table, one with numerous small pieces of different varieties of bagels, and the other with larger pieces of different bagels. The residents were asked to take and eat as many as they wanted, and then to evaluate how much they enjoyed the bagels. What the researchers were really interested in was how many small and how many large pieces each person took. The findings were similar to the results of the two studies just discussed: those in the low-power group (whose banner said that we feel powerless in the morning) took more large pieces than those in the other two groups. However, there was no difference in the number of small pieces; the only difference was in the number of large pieces of bagels taken. Since the bagels were free, this study demonstrates that the association between a powerful feeling and the size of a product is not necessarily due to the product's price.

The results suggest that the size of a chosen product signals status, even when the product itself has nothing to do with power and status. We all know that bigger cars and houses are status symbols, but these findings demonstrate that this association holds true for products that, on their own, are totally unrelated to power and status. Apparently, we gauge status not only by the size of someone's car or house but also by the size of her or his coffee. And sometimes a bigger cup of coffee might compensate for the fact that, at a particular moment, nobody is listening to us.

Take a Stand – Power Yourself Up

'It's not the size of the dog in the fight, it's the size of the fight in the dog,' said Mark Twain.

We humans assume powerful and powerless poses across different cultures using size and vertical positioning. We have seen that animals display dominance by spreading their limbs and taking up more space. Similarly, a powerful person may choose to stand, legs and arms spread, expanding in space. A submissive person might sit, head bowed, hands held close to the body, and legs together in order to shrink as much as possible, as do abused children and prisoners of war.

Besides conveying power or weakness, is it possible that our postures influence the way we judge ourselves? Can power itself be embodied? Can the state of sitting or standing in a given position influence how powerful or powerless we feel? A group of researchers investigated this question, dividing participants in the study into two groups.[23] Each group was asked to pose for two minutes. Those in the 'power-pose' group were asked to stand and then to sit with their hands spread on the table and legs apart. Those in the low-power group were asked to sit down and later to stand with their hands around their bodies or between their knees, legs close together, limbs closed, and taking up as little space as possible.

The researchers conducted a pretest to make sure that neither pose was more or less uncomfortable or difficult. Participants were unaware of the study's true objective and were told that the experiment was examining how the placement of electrocardiography electrodes influences data collection. The researchers relied on several criteria to quantify how powerful the participants felt.

The first measure was the simplest – they just asked participants how powerful they felt. Those who displayed high-power poses reported feeling more powerful than those who displayed low-power poses. The second measure gauged risk-taking behaviour, because when people feel more powerful they are more likely to take risks. Each participant received two dollars and could either pocket the money or use it to gamble, with a chance of either losing the two dollars or doubling the sum. In other words, the participants could play it safe or take a risk. Eighty-six per cent of participants in the power-pose group gambled, whereas only 60 per cent of the low-power group took the risk. Merely posing for a couple of minutes in a powerful or powerless position caused participants to feel more or less powerful and influenced their risk-taking behaviour.

The researchers did not just measure participants' feelings of power and their risk-taking behaviour; they actually measured powerful feeling physiologically by taking saliva samples immediately after participants finished sitting or standing in their respective poses, and testing the saliva for two hormones: testosterone and cortisol. Testosterone is positively correlated with dominant (i.e. powerful) behaviour. High levels of testosterone increase dominant behaviour, and, reciprocally, dominant behaviour increases testosterone levels. Cortisol is a stress hormone; people who feel powerful tend to have lower levels of cortisol than those who feel powerless.

The results showed that those who were sitting and standing in high-power poses for two minutes had an increased level of testosterone and a decreased level of cortisol. In contrast, those who sat or stood in low-power positions demonstrated decreased testosterone levels and increased cortisol levels. These results lend major scientific support to embodiment theory. The hormone-level test results demonstrate that there is a clear association between our bodily positions and our feelings and behaviour. Our bodies influence our minds. Simple postures can convey feelings of physical power as well as mental strength. We actually come to feel more emotionally powerful through the way our bodies feel physically.

You can use this knowledge. Adjust your posture, movements and mannerisms not only to project power but also to give yourself more feelings of confidence and efficacy. If you are feeling timid or unassertive, stand or sit in 'power poses' to bolster your mental state. If you want to boost your confidence at a job interview; on a first date; or when joining a new group, showing up alone at a party where you don't know anyone, or anticipating a difficult family meeting, just stand in a powerful pose for a few minutes before you enter a room (and while you're interacting). You can change how you feel about yourself as well as your consequent behaviour and the way others perceive you.

When our parents or our teachers told us to sit up straight, most of us didn't take them very seriously. But keeping your back straight really does influence your feelings of power and your behaviour as well as what others think of you. Standing straight is good not only for the back but also for the soul!

Conclusions and Implications

Even abstract concepts are grounded in our perceptual and bodily experiences. Power is grounded in our perceptual experiences of both vertical positioning and size. The concept of power is represented in our minds along a vertical continuum, and it also takes into account the size and the volume of an object or another person. All the metaphors we've noted that use vertical positioning to depict status and power are more than just means of enriching our language. In fact, when we think of a person's high status, our attention shifts upward.

You can use the findings in this chapter to appear and feel more powerful. Height is directly related to power perception, and most women know the power of a good pair of heels. Although it's no easy trick to genuinely elevate our status and influence in the world, if we combine all of the little tricks this body of research has taught us – like using high ground, picture angles, projections of stature, and body postures – together with some common sense, we can influence others' perceptions of us. We can appear, like my grandfather, larger than life. Knowing this association between physical and psychological concepts, we also become far less susceptible to being influenced by a tall person or an upper-floor office. We can use these findings to deconstruct others' attempts to influence us and to recognise subtle influences that may have swayed us unconsciously in the past.

Postures and poses matter. Try not to sit on a chair that places you lower than others around you in business or social interactions. This is especially important in interactions that involve negotiations, high-stakes conversations, or first dates. It is also true for group projects where, on the surface, all partners seem to be endowed with the same power and responsibility. Be mindful of your position when sitting on the floor in a group, be mindful of your posture, and be mindful in general of the message you send by the space and level you occupy.

Like many other findings in embodied cognition, these studies also point up our own biases and sometimes unfair judgements of other people. Remember that you have inherited an automatic bias associating size and vertical positioning with power, and with positivity and negativity. We often attribute positive or negative characteristics to people when in fact we are biased by vertical positioning. Whenever you find yourself judging others who are tall or short, or when you view photos that have been taken from different angles, devote a few seconds to deconstructing your impression and consider what has influenced your initial reaction. Being aware of these associations can help you minimise their untoward influence.

No matter what your height, the research is clear: perceptions of both height and position are tools that anyone can use in order to influence perceptions of power and status.

9

Out, Damned Spot:
Guilt, Morality and Cleaning

. . . .

Cleanliness is next to godliness.

PROVERB

. . . .

It was the winter of 1989 and I was teaching Introduction to Psychology at Harvard University. December in Cambridge was a new experience for me, and my time had been divided between conducting my research, teaching, taking care of my children, and trying not to freeze. In short, I needed a vacation. Fortunately, a friend of mine called to ask if we wanted to join her on a two-day ski trip to Vermont. The hotel, she said quietly, as if she were revealing some great secret, was *free of charge*. All we had to do, she assured me, was attend a three-hour lecture and demonstration during which the sponsoring company would try to sell us a timeshare unit. The psychologist in me was suspicious, but my friend assured me that we definitely wouldn't have to buy. We would show up, sip coffee and nod politely, then slip off to the slopes and get a desperately needed, utterly free vacation.

So we ventured north, cars over-packed, four families with kids heading for the slopes.

We arrived at a posh little ski resort and the following morning, after breakfast, were herded into a large room. Each couple sat separately with a smiling salesman who had papers at the ready. Our salesman slid into a well-practised sales pitch about all the beautiful places we could go and the money we could save if we would only step up and embrace the joys of timeshare property ownership. I'll admit it looked enticing to be able to go to various places in the world and stay in a very nice unit that would cost us no more than our regular vacations. Through the salesman's focused lens, I saw the appeal.

Today, far from that ski lodge, I don't remember most of the details, locations, or prices, or even what our salesman looked like. But I do remember this: he had an angry red stain on his white shirtsleeve, probably strawberry jam, that demanded my attention through his entire pitch. I felt that he was unclean, and I was turned off by the deal. After two hours of stain gazing, we politely said no and went on our way.

One of the other couples we had come with wanted to buy a unit. When my friends challenged me about my reservations, I couldn't really articulate a good answer; I just *felt* it wasn't a good deal. The figures the company presented made sense, the photos were all beautiful, and the locales all spoke for buying. In the following years I would hear about people who felt trapped in their timeshare units and were trying to get out of their contracts, but on that winter morning at the ski resort, I was unaware of any negative information.

I just felt as if the deal had a stain on it.

I am sure there were many reasons we did not buy the unit, but one of them was how I perceived the credibility of the salesman and the company he represented. I didn't see him as reliable. It doesn't seem very logical that the stain on his shirt that kept my rapt attention during our conversation could have represented his honesty. After all, investment decisions are not made on the basis of how wrinkled or dirty the salesman's shirt is or whether he smells nice, right?

Maybe not. Studies suggest, though, that, without even being aware of it, we associate morality with physical cleanliness, and we associate it powerfully.

Cleansing the Soul: Rituals in Language, Religion and Art

Across cultures and in almost every religion, people often speak about issues of morality in terms of cleanliness. Expressions such as *clean conscience, dirty work* and *wash away sins* all demonstrate the metaphorical link between ethical behaviour and physical cleansing. Christians baptise their children so that they 'should no longer be slaves of sin' (Romans 6:6). Judaism requires bathing in a special place, called a 'mikveh', for ritual purity, and ritual bathing is discussed in detail in the Bible. In Islam, it is customary to wash before prayer. Hindus bathe in the holy river Ganges to wash away their sins.

Some gurus instruct those seeking to cleanse their souls to visualise the spiritual detritus they want to be rid of as mud and grime and to visualise washing away that dirt with water. Many psychologists believe that obsessive-compulsive disorder, which includes ritual hand washing, may result from fear of contamination and be related to feelings of mental pollution and guilt.

Francis Ford Coppola's classic film *The Godfather* depicts the complicated lives of a crime family: the Corleones. At the beginning of the film, Michael Corleone (Al Pacino), a son of the ageing Mafia boss, is a clean-cut American war hero whom the family intends to keep out of its nefarious business. But when his older brother, Sonny (James Caan), is assassinated and his father, the godfather (Marlon

Brando), dies, Michael becomes the family's leader and head of the syndicate, completing his transformation into the godfather.

Towards the end of the film, Michael attends the baptism of his infant son. The action cuts from the church, with the priest chanting Latin prayers, to assassins preparing their vehicles, disguises and weapons. As Michael is asked, 'Do you renounce Satan?' and replies, 'I do renounce him,' we see a series of murders of Michael's enemies. The holy scene of the baptism is deliberately juxtaposed with gruesome violence and, as water is finally poured over the head of the infant, we are meant to see the contradiction between salvation and sin. A man who was once pure becomes baptised with blood into a life of violence, renouncing his former innocence. Good and evil both exist, and Coppola uses water, with all its cleansing associations, and blood, with its vengeful and sacrificial connotations, to set up this essential moral contradiction.

Who Keeps It Clean?

The pervasive associations between cleanliness and morality are not just metaphors and artistic inventions, however. We really do associate physical cleaning with morality. Several researchers have explored these questions with fascinating results.

Chen-Bo Zhong and Katie Liljenquist examined whether those who feel a threat to their moral selves have a greater urge to clean themselves, and therefore place a higher value on cleansing-related objects.[1] In their first experiment, the researchers invited 60 students from Northwestern University to their laboratory and randomly assigned them to two groups. The students in one group were asked to recall an unethical act, such as a lie or misdeed, from their past and to describe their emotions about it. The students in the other group were asked to recall an ethical act – taking responsibility or telling the truth – and to describe how they felt about it. Students were told that this was a study investigating memories associated with ethical and unethical behaviour. Then, in an ostensibly separate study, these same students were asked to participate in a word-completion task. The task consisted of series of incomplete words, such as 's - - p', 'sh - - er' and 'w - - h', that had to be made into complete words by filling in the blanks. Some words could be completed in several ways, but one of the possibilities was cleansing related. For example, 's - - p' could be completed as *soap*, a cleansing word, but it could also be completed as *ship*, *slip*, *slap*, *stop*, or *step*, words totally unrelated to cleansing. The results clearly indicated that those who recalled an unethical deed completed the words as cleansing-related ones more often than did people who recalled an ethical deed.

In a second experiment, the researchers again asked participants to recall an ethical or an unethical deed. However, this time they asked participants to choose a free gift, either an antiseptic wipe or a pencil (the choices were found to be equally desirable in a pretest). Remarkably, 67 per cent of the participants who thought about an unethical deed chose the antiseptic wipe, while only 33 per cent of those who thought about the ethical deed chose this gift.

In a third study, the researchers asked a group of undergraduate students to hand-copy a typeset story written in the first person, telling them that the experiment was about the connection between hand-writing and personality. The students were then randomly divided into two groups. Students in the first group, the 'ethical' group, were asked to hand-copy a story about an honest office worker in competition with a colleague, and students in the second group, the 'unethical' group, were asked to hand-copy a story about an office worker, also in competition with a colleague, who had done something underhanded. Although the participants were only copying the story, it was written in the first person and so would make them identify with the character telling it.

The 'ethical man' story was about a lawyer who found a misplaced document that was much needed by a colleague in order to successfully argue a case and did the right thing – he placed it on his colleague's desk, without even taking credit for his kind deed. The 'unethical man' story was about a lawyer who found the same missing document but kept mum and shredded the document, thus ensuring his colleague's failure and paving the way for his own promotion.

Here's the clever part: the students were then asked, in a supposedly different study, to rate the desirability of several products on a seven-point scale. Some of the products were cleansing products, such as toothpaste, soap and laundry detergent; there were also unrelated products, such as fruit juice, CD cases and Snickers bars. Those who copied the story about the unethical worker found the cleansing-related items more desirable than did those who copied the ethical story. No difference was found in ratings of the products unrelated to cleansing. After the simple act of handwriting a first-person account about an unethical deed, participants demonstrated greater interest in self-cleansing. The participants acted as if some of the 'psychological scum' of the unethical lawyer could be scrubbed off by physical cleaning.

These three studies present an interesting notion of 'mental cleanliness'. Our unethical deeds may really cling to our psyches like a layer of grime, making us feel the urge to wash ourselves until we are pure again. At the very least, the findings show that our misdeeds (and even misdeeds that aren't ours) linger in our minds and have an effect on us.

Psychologists and psychiatrists have coined the term *mental pollution* to describe a feeling of dirtiness that may be caused by unethical deeds or thoughts, moral criticism, or physical or sexual assault. People who feel they are mentally polluted often want to clean themselves.

Canadian researchers asked a group of female students to imagine a non-consensual kiss at a party and asked another group to imagine a consensual kiss.[2] Those who imagined the non-consensual kiss felt dirtier, and some wanted to wash out their mouths. The students who imagined a consensual kiss did not have these reactions. Although the non-consensual kiss was only imaginary, even the thought of it was enough to make the women feel polluted.

A magazine reporter interviewed young mothers who worked as prostitutes during the day, while their children were at school or in the nursery.[3] Most of the women were single mothers who sold sex in order to pay their bills and support their children. A social worker who knew them well said that at the end of the day most of them washed and cleaned themselves as if to purify themselves. The act meant more to them than just physical cleaning. They felt polluted by their day's work and cleaned themselves for a very long time before allowing themselves to return to their children.

Naughty Parts: The Body Broken Down by Guilt

We use different parts of our bodies to perform unethical acts. People lie and swear with their mouths, steal with their hands, and run away on their legs even when staying would be the right thing to do. Other body parts, which we need not discuss in detail, are famous for getting men and women (even presidents and heads of armed forces) into all manner of moral and ethical quandaries.

In 1993 the case of John and Lorena Bobbitt, a Virginia couple, received a lot of media attention. John had an alleged history of abuse and infidelity, and one night he returned home from a party, intoxicated, and allegedly raped his wife while she was sleeping. Lorena went to the kitchen, got a knife, and cut off nearly half of her husband's penis. Why did she punish him in such a way?

Historically, religions have linked the ethical quality of certain actions with the body parts that perform them. Both the Bible and the Quran punish the particular part of the body involved in unethical behaviour. They demand localised suffering. The Bible says: 'May the LORD cut off all flattering lips, the tongue that speaketh proud things' (Psalms 12:3). And in Proverbs, it is written: 'From the mouth of the righteous comes the fruit of wisdom, but a perverse tongue will be silenced' (10:31).

In the Quran, theft is punished by imprisonment, but in extreme cases by amputation of hands. 'As for the man who steals and the woman who steals,' it says, 'cut off the hand of either of them in requital for what they have wrought, as a deterrent ordained by God: for God is almighty, wise' (5:38).

Although theft is punished by amputation only in extreme cases, the message is there. The punishment is designed to fit the part of the body that committed the crime. Freud coined the term *castration anxiety* to refer to the unconscious fear of a boy who, at an early stage of his development, is attracted to his mother and sees his father as his rival. According to Freud, the boy associates the punishment, castration, with the body part involved in the sin.

Is it possible that people not only want to clean themselves after immoral behaviour but also want to clean the specific part of the body that was involved in this moral transgression? If our abstract concepts are grounded in our bodily experiences, then it is likely that cleansing is related to the specific action or motor behaviour. To measure this association, researchers asked 87 students to imagine that they were working as lawyers and competing with a colleague.[4] As in the study about honest and unethical actions, the lawyer finds a crucially important document belonging to a competitor. The participant then is asked to deliver an unethical message to the colleague – a lie stating that he or she had not found the document. Half of the students delivered the message via voicemail, and the other half via e-mail.

Like the other studies, this one had an 'unrelated' product survey, in which the researchers asked the students to rate the desirability of various products. Among the several products were two in which the researchers were most interested: mouthwash and hand sanitiser. Students who delivered the unethical message via e-mail, and therefore used their hands, found the hand sanitiser more desirable. In contrast, students who delivered the lie via voicemail, and therefore used their mouths, found the mouthwash more desirable. The test subjects wanted to clean the part of the body with which they had told a lie. It seems that just as we want to wash our hands and feet after they touch something dirty, we feel the need to clean the exact body part involved in a moral transgression.

Cruel punishments like amputations do not exist in most civilised countries today, but associations between body parts and their deeds remain in the public conscience. On blogs, where more deviant impulses, whether political, legal, or social, can still be expressed anonymously, it is not hard to find calls for embodied revenge. For example, several bloggers suggested that the tongue of a woman who falsely accused someone of attacking her should be amputated. Despite our cultural modernity, the minds of many of us are still prone to making these automatic connections. Plus, who can ever forget the most well-known threatened punishment for cursing, voiced by parents and schoolteachers: 'I'm going to wash your mouth out with soap!' There is an embodied reason this threat may never go out of style.

Does Cleaning Make Us Feel Morally Pure?

While we know that we have a greater urge to clean ourselves when we do something immoral, does this unconscious compensation really work? Does physical cleaning really cleanse our conscience and wash away our guilty feelings? Can you lie to a friend, then wash your hands (or, even better, your mouth) and feel somewhat better about the whole thing?

Zhong and Liljenquist conducted another experiment that explored this question.[5] Undergraduate students were asked to recall an unethical deed and type it into a computer. Immediately afterward half of the students were asked to wipe their hands with an antiseptic cleansing wipe and were told that this action was recommended after using someone else's keyboard. The other half were not asked to clean their hands. Subsequently, all the participants were asked if they would help a desperate graduate student by volunteering to take part in a study without pay. The researchers assumed people who had the lingering feeling that they had done something immoral or unethical would feel guilty and therefore would try to compensate for their act by doing a good deed, such as volunteering.

Indeed, they found that 74 per cent of those who did not clean their hands volunteered to help, while only 41 per cent of those who had cleaned their hands volunteered. For those who had cleaned their hands, that simple act was enough to abate the feelings of guilt that had been brought up by recalling the unethical deed. They'd already 'cleaned' their conscience. For those who did not clean their hands, the urge to soothe that guilt pushed them to volunteer at a much higher rate. These results suggest that physical cleaning indeed clears our conscience.

I further investigated this question with my students at Tel Aviv University.* We wondered whether people who are physically clean have a higher tolerance for cheating and committing other dubious acts. Basically, we posited that you have more 'room' for moral dirt when your physical 'slate' is clean.

---

* Yaniv Golan and Shani Busnach.

In our study, two students went to the university gym and stood near the door leading to the shower stalls in order to approach two groups of people: people who had just finished working out and were on their way to the showers and those who had just finished showering. Each person was asked to participate in a short study and was told that the study examined the influence of physical training on memory.

Participants from both groups received 'general knowledge' questionnaires composed of thirteen questions. Nine of the questions were extremely difficult, bordering on impossible to answer, while four were very easy. We had assembled these questions from earlier research (a pretest). In the pretest we had asked students to answer some easy and some very difficult questions. We chose for the easy questions on the shower test those that pretest takers had unanimously answered correctly, and we chose as difficult questions those that not even one of the pretest participants had answered even partially correctly. For example, one of our easy questions was 'How many centimetres are there in one metre?' while one of our difficult questions was 'In what year was the stethoscope invented?' We chose a ratio of four easy and nine difficult to ensure that participants would get a failing score (four easy questions out of thirteen is about 30 per cent).

We chose to measure cheating by enabling participants to self-score their tests. Each participant was given the correct answer key, asked to check her or his answers, and instructed to write the score on a separate page. After this, participants would hand over to the experimenter only the last page, on which they had written their scores, and tear up their original tests and put them in the recycling bin. Participants were certain that there was no way for the administrators of the test to determine their actual performance. They felt free to misreport. They didn't know that we didn't need to see the tests to know their scores, those cheaters.

Those who answered the questionnaire before the shower, when they were still sweaty, cheated less than those who answered the questionnaire after the shower, when they felt clean. Our study confirmed that those who felt clean on the outside felt 'clean' enough on the inside to be able to falsify their test scores and report that they had correctly answered some of the impossible questions. It was as if they felt a 'morality surplus' while clean, as if they had moral character to spare and could thus cheat.

In a second study that I conducted with my student* we wanted to examine whether cleansing for the purpose of purification would influence donation behaviour. We conducted this study in the mikveh, the traditional Jewish communal bath for purification, on two special days: the Jewish New Year (Rosh Hashanah) and the Day of Atonement (Yom Kippur). The ten days between these two holidays are called the High Holy Days, or the Days of Awe. According to the Jewish tradition, on New Year's Day God writes in the book of life the names of those who will live and those who will die, and he seals it with the verdict on the Day of Atonement, the holiest day of the year. This period is therefore a time for soul-searching, during which believers seek to make amends and ask for forgiveness for wrongdoing. Observers also go to wash in the mikveh to purify themselves. Another tradition in the Days of Awe is charity; representatives of various organisations commonly set up stands outside the mikveh asking for donations from the visitors.

We examined whether men were likely to donate more before washing themselves in the mikveh or after. We predicted that those who were on their way to the mikveh would have a greater need for purification and would therefore donate more money than those who had just purified themselves.

We situated ourselves a few metres from the entrance and exit of

---

* Shimon Malov.

the mikveh with the stand of a real charitable organisation that distributes food to the needy. We set up a table with flyers presenting information about the organisation's activities and open boxes where people could put their financial donations. A volunteer who was blind to the purpose of the study manned the table and wrote down the sum of each donation and whether the person had donated before or after washing. And we did indeed find that people donated more before they washed than after they washed in the mikveh.

These results might seem counter-intuitive. You might think that when your body is clean, your moral behaviour would be clean as well. However, intuition alone cannot unravel the web of connections between our senses and our minds. Our findings suggest that physical cleaning influences moral transgressions. Physical cleanliness is relative, and the moral mechanism seems to operate only when we become cleaner than we were. As we've seen, physical cleansing reduces guilt.

Physical dirtiness is conceptually and metaphorically linked to immorality. By cleaning themselves and removing the dirt, individuals cleansed their conscience, thereby granting themselves licence to cheat and decreasing the impulse to help others. With a clean conscience and less guilt, individuals seem able to commit at least minor moral transgressions more easily. Something about being physically clean resonates with the psyche, indicating to the conscience that a person has a moral 'clean slate' that can afford some smudging. It is as if, by cleaning their conscience, participants had more 'slack' to commit moral transgressions. In contrast, when we are physically unclean, we seem to have a lower tolerance for our own misdeeds and are more sensitive to guilt. We associate physical dirt with an unclean conscience and so do not allow ourselves to further transgress. These phenomena, the way the mind and body affect each other, are what embodiment is about.

Disgust, Cleanliness and Moral Judgement

What determines moral judgements? Why is one behaviour judged harshly while another is forgiven? Why is the same act perceived by one person as benign and by another as a serious moral transgression that deserves harsh punishment? There is no doubt that our values, upbringing, perspectives and personalities influence our moral judgements, but some situational variables also bend and adjust them. Can a simple environmental factor, like the cleanliness of a room or its smell, affect our judgements? Does physical disgust lead us to be morally disgusted and harsher in our judgements? Indeed, recent research has started to link our capacity for disgust to our moral views.

Early in life we begin to register physical disgust evoked by rotten foods and bad smells. Evolutionary psychologists believe that physical disgust is an adaptation that developed early in our evolution to keep us away from disease-causing organisms. We are revolted by guts and gore because contact with them can make us sick. But behaviours unrelated to disease also disgust us, and researchers believe that there is a link between disgust related to diseases and moral disgust. Some behaviours that have little to do with the avoidance of infection are often described using the language of disgust. They may actually leave a bad taste in the mouth. For instance, we feel disgusted when we hear about a man who betrayed his best friend or when we hear of murder, adultery and incest. Physical disgust and moral disgust produce similar vocal and facial expressions and activate some of the same brain regions, which indicate that they might influence one another.[6]

Several studies have recently examined whether disgust evoked by physical factors such as bad smells or contaminated objects influences how wrong we think certain moral transgressions are. These studies induced physical disgust by various means and then presented participants with scenarios describing moral transgressions or dilemmas and asked them to judge how wrong these issues were. In one study the experimenters sprayed a disgusting smell, a fart spray (in the name of science), not far from the participants while they were answering the questionnaire.[7] In another study the participants drank a disgustingly bitter drink.[8] The moral transgressions included vignettes about stealing library books, offering a bribe and shoplifting. The moral dilemmas included issues such as sex and legalisation of marriage between first cousins. Some of the studies included a scenario about a man eating his own dead dog.

The results clearly demonstrated that those who were physically disgusted (by smelling a disgusting smell or tasting a disgusting drink) were harsher in their moral judgements compared with those who were not exposed to bad odours or who drank sweet or neutral drinks. In other words, the same behaviour was judged as more morally wrong if the person who made the judgement was subjected to unpleasant odours or a disgusting drink. Physical disgust influenced moral disgust. It's as if the human brain can be 'made ready' to feel or generate moral disgust by triggering the evolutionary process of physical disgust.

Yet it is possible that washing hands will wash away this influence of disgust on moral judgement. A group of researchers induced disgust in their participants by showing them a repulsive movie clip, after which half of the participants washed their hands.[9] All participants were then asked to judge several behaviours. Those who had washed their hands after watching the disgusting film clip judged immoral behaviour less harshly than did those who did not wash their hands. The cleaning seemed to rinse away their disgust or at least its influence.

These results suggest that physical disgust influences us to make harsher moral judgements, while physical cleaning influences to judge moral issues less harshly. Two different studies examined the latter phenomenon and came up with seemingly contradictory results. In one study a group of British researchers[10] presented students with four scrambled sentences, which they were to form into meaningful sentences. For one group, half of the sentences had words that were related to purity or cleanliness, such as *clean, washed* and *pure*. The other group received only neutral sentences without any cleaning-related words. The participants were then asked to judge several moral dilemmas. Those who read cleaning-related words were less harsh in their moral judgements than those who read neutral words. Just reading words like *wash, clean* and *pure* in sentences activated concepts of cleanliness and consequently made participants think less harshly about others' immoral behaviour.

In the other study,[11] the researchers manipulated cleaning not by letting their participants read cleaning-related words but by asking participants in one group to cleanse their hands with an antiseptic wipe before they touched the computer, and comparing their judgements with those by a group who did not clean their hands.

In contrast to the previous study, researchers found that those who washed their hands judged various social dilemmas as more morally wrong than did those who did not wash their hands.

But these seemingly contradictory results might not be so different. In the first study the participants were thinking about clean words and may have applied this cleaning concept to the moral issues, consequently judging them less harshly. In the second study the participants *cleaned themselves* and felt pure and clean, consequently judging other moral issues more harshly. The link between physical cleaning and morality is complex, but seemingly irrelevant things, such as experiencing a bad smell or taste, having clean hands, or reading clean words, can influence how wrong certain transgressions seem to us.

This is quite a disturbing finding. We would like to believe that our moral judgements are determined by our bedrock values and that we decide that an act is morally wrong according to those values, not by the smell of the room or whether the room is clean or messy.

How Does It Work?

This link between physical cleaning and morality may be explained from both an evolutionary and a metaphorical perspective. As mentioned in the previous section, physical disgust probably developed to protect us from germs, parasites, and other carriers of disease. The disgust reaction is aversion, which makes us avoid the causes of our disgust. Emotions of moral disgust developed later, out of the physical disgust we experience, and often are described using the language of disgust.

This link can also be explained by scaffolding, the association between concrete concepts and abstract concepts. Metaphors link the abstract and concrete domains, and abstract concepts are grounded in the concrete concepts that we experience through our senses. Our notion of morality is grounded in the experience of physical disgust and cleanliness that we learn early in life.

I was driving with a friend of mine and three children: my three-year-old granddaughter, Natalie; and my friend's two grandchildren, a four-and-a-half-year-old boy and an eight-year-old girl. The two older children were talking about a game they like, and Natalie was trying valiantly to get a word in edgewise. When she finally got her chance, she said: 'You know what is yucky? Poop!' The four-and-a-half-year-old boy sitting next to her retorted: 'You know what is also yucky? A rotten banana!'

It is easy for a grandmother to be entertained by her granddaughter, but what occupied three-year-old Natalie's mind to prompt her to say that she was disgusted by 'poop'? Perhaps she was also disgusted by being excluded. Once on the playground I heard a five-year-old boy call another boy he was angry at 'poop'. Like warmth and affection, disgust seems to be built into our psyches.

The emotions of moral disgust are scaffolded onto the reactions and emotions of physical disgust. As we grow, our understanding and context of moral disgust is based in the same physical reaction of disgust we have known all our lives. Evolution has created a shortcut to help us understand and feel complex moral concepts. That's why it's natural for us to call an immoral person 'rotten to the core' or a 'filthy liar'.

The Moral of the Story

We have the desire to clean ourselves after unethical deeds, so be aware if you notice more frequent and longer washing habits in your children or partners. They may be just the first indication that you ought to look more carefully at possible reasons and connections. Guilt is a very personal experience. For many, guilt is reconciliation, a necessary process that we feel obliged to experience when we've done something wrong or less than ethical. But if you are having a hard time letting go of guilt, a conscious act of washing yourself can help you release some of those feelings and move on.

Another important implication of these studies relates to our habits and decisions as consumers. If indeed we associate cleanliness with morality, then it follows that we probably perceive a cleaner environment as more ethical. That it is more pleasant to be in a clean environment than in a dirty one is news to no one. Most people would agree that it is more pleasant to do business in a clean and tidy room than in a messy one. This notion is as true for a computer store as it is for a doctor's clinic. The studies just discussed, however, go a step further, suggesting that without our awareness, we perceive a company and its representatives as more ethical, reliable and honest in a clean environment than in a less clean one.

Quite often we find ourselves in situations where we have to decide whether to buy a certain product, or to choose between several professionals, such as doctors, dentists, or repair persons. Sometimes we face these decisions armed with recommendations from our friends, but often we don't have a clue.

I think we can all agree that sometimes what salespeople tell you is true, sometimes it's an exaggeration, and sometimes it's an outright lie. One of the most important factors in the sale is how reliable and honest the company or the salesperson seems. If the environment (e.g. shop, office, clinic) is clean and has a tidy aesthetic; if the salespeople radiate cleanliness, smell nice, and are dressed in clean, fresh-looking clothes; if the location is clean and smells fresh, there is a better chance that we will believe what we are told. It's easy to be suspicious if the store or clinic is filthy, messy and ill-kempt. While we cannot control our unconscious inclinations, being aware of our susceptibility to these environmental factors could help us to exercise caution the next time we are being given a hard sell. A neat salesperson is not necessarily honest, and a frumpy, dishevelled one need not necessarily be regarded with suspicion. Moreover, a cleaner salesperson may be more likely to cheat, and a dirty homeless person could be the most honest person you meet.

Cleanliness isn't a magic trick that can wash away guilt or make a sale. It is, however, another inch in a game of inches, and another facet of the mind to understand and be aware of. Most of us do associate morality and cleanliness. Our moral judgements and behaviour, which we may hold as absolute, are nonetheless affected by these unconscious connections. Washing hands is about more than just preparing for dinner; expressions such as *dirty hands, dirty mouth* and *clean conscience* are not just figures of speech. These findings are both interesting and important to our understanding of how the mind works and how close our sensory and bodily sensations are to our emotions, behaviours and judgements.

Water Under the Bridge

My parents, probably my greatest teachers, used to tell me an old story about a very poor man who lived in a small house with his wife and six children. The family was in dire financial straits and found it taxing to live all together in one small room. Near his breaking point, the man went to seek the advice of his rabbi. After listening to the man tell of the difficulties of living in such a small space, the rabbi asked the man if he kept animals in the yard. The man said he had a cow, a goat and chickens. The rabbi's advice was to move the animals into the house. The man, surprised as he was, did as the rabbi told him to do. A few days later, the man came back to the rabbi, reporting that his family's situation had worsened. The rabbi's advice was to remove the chickens. Another few days went by, and the man returned once more, complaining about the mess that the cow and the goat were making. The rabbi's advice? Take the cow out, and then a few days later do the same with the goat. The man came to the rabbi and thanked him profusely, telling him that life was much easier now.

This story has many morals, but the one I want to emphasise is that the past influences how we see the present, and everything is relative. The present looked much better when the recent past was bad, when the tiny house was filled with not only six children but also chickens, a cow and a goat. Having reverted to the original circumstances, which had seemed unbearable only a few weeks earlier, the man perceived his situation as good.

Can washing or cleaning – as in 'wiping the slate clean' – wash away the influence of past events, behaviours, or emotions? The past influences our present.

The idea that water washes away the past is deeply rooted in the human psyche. One need only look to the prevalence of flood narratives in ancient civilisations. There is, of course, the well-known Old Testament story of Noah and the Ark, in which God, having learned of the evils of human civilisation, instructs Noah to build an ark large enough to save only his immediate family and a pair of every species of animal before God floods the Earth until it is cleansed. Earlier stories offer similar narratives of a divinely ordained 'great flood' and a heroic man instructed by a deity to build a great vessel in order to survive the deluge. In the Mesopotamian Epic of Gilgamesh, Utnapishtim recounts to Gilgamesh how the god Ea warned him of an impending flood. In the Satapatha Brahmana, a Hindu text, Manu is warned by the god Vishnu (in the form of a fish) to build a boat and prepare for a devastating flood. A common thread uniting these narratives is the notion that wicked human behaviour prompted a divine entity to wash away all traces of civilisation and wipe the slate clean.

To examine whether water can wash away psychological pain from the past, Norbert Schwarz and his colleagues conducted several experiments. Their first study used *cognitive dissonance*, which is the discomfort we experience when we hold conflicting beliefs, values, or ideas, to explore how our respective 'slates' are cleaned.[12]

A little background on cognitive dissonance. We are constantly faced with choices. We decide what to buy, where to go, whom to date or marry, where to live, which doctor to visit, where we or our kids will attend school, what table we want in our dining room. It is often difficult to choose between two alternatives, but life demands that we make a decision, and thus we do. Nevertheless, the second alternative – the one we did not choose – might still be attractive, lingering in the back of the mind. These conflicting thoughts cause cognitive dissonance.

Theoretically, we loss-averse humans could agonise over our decisions forever, but this would only lead to discomfort – and our minds have evolved to avoid that outcome. Once we make a decision, typically we will strongly justify our choice and decide, for instance, that the car we purchased is much more attractive, well suited to us, and generally better than the other car we considered, when in reality both had advantages and disadvantages.

Our past decisions influence the way we perceive choices. Once we've made a decision, in order to reduce the cognitive dissonance, our brains favour the chosen alternative compared with the rejected one.

Back to the 'clean slate' experiment. To test whether physical washing would eliminate this lingering influence of previous decisions, the researchers presented students with 30 music CDs and asked them to select ten that they liked, ranking them in order of preference, with the number 1 being the best liked. As a thank-you gift, they were then offered one CD and asked to decide between their fifth and sixth choices.

After the students made their choices, the researchers asked them to participate in another, ostensibly different marketing study, in which they were to evaluate a liquid soap. Half of the students were asked to examine the bottle of the soap, while the other half were asked to actually wash their hands with the soap.

At the third stage of the study, the researchers asked the students to rank again the same ten CDs they had ranked in the first part of the study. For those who did not wash their hands, the perceived difference between the chosen and the unchosen CD increased. They behaved as expected, and acted in accordance with a belief that could be expressed as: 'You know what, this CD is pretty good, I was right to choose it, I'm gonna rank it higher this time.' A CD, once chosen, rose in value because of that choice. However, those who washed their hands after making their choice did not change their preference, and the difference between the ranking of the CD they chose and the one not chosen did not increase. They did not feel the need to justify their choices by preferring the chosen CD more than the one not chosen. The simple act of washing seemed to wipe away the influence of the previous decision.

The researchers conducted a comparable study to see whether the results could be replicated. They presented participants with photos of four different fruit jams and asked them to evaluate each jam as part of a consumer survey. They then asked them to choose one of two jams as a thank-you gift. Then the researchers asked the participants to evaluate an antiseptic wipe. In that regard this study was similar to the first study: half of the participants just examined the wipe, whereas the other half cleaned their hands with it. Finally they were asked to rate the expected tastes of the four jams. As in the previous study, the effect of cognitive dissonance was clearly found in those who did not clean their hands. They expected the chosen jam to taste much better than the jam they did not choose and needed to justify their choice. This effect was not observed in those participants who had cleaned their hands. The researchers called this the *clean-slate effect*. These results suggest that even a cursory cleaning minimises the influence of past decisions.

This finding raises the possibility that cleaning may decrease or even eliminate the influence of not only cognitive dissonance but also other past events. Norbert Schwarz and his colleagues examined whether the simple act of cleaning would eliminate the impact of previous good or bad luck on future risk taking.[13]

Most of us face the dilemma of how much risk to allow in various spheres of our lives. The classic example is investments. We can simply hold on to our money, invest in a safe bet that gives a very small percentage return per year, or buy stocks that may give us higher profits with a potential for great losses. My investment consultant always asks me how much risk I am willing to take. Would I like to invest in equity at a rate of 10 per cent, 30 per cent, or 50 per cent? If I say 50 per cent, I am assuming a bigger risk; I have a chance of making a better profit, but also a greater chance to lose. The same principle applies to real estate. One dilemma investors commonly face is whether to buy a given property while the market is down. It seems like a good investment, since there is a good chance that prices will go up. Nevertheless, there is a risk associated with the purchase since prices may continue to go down. Some people are willing to take that risk, win or lose, and others simply are not.

Many factors are at play in determining how great a risk we want to take, including, of course, our personalities. One of those factors is how lucky we feel. I once put 50 per cent of my assets in an equity investment and lost almost all of it. I had taken a big risk and gotten burned. For a long time I felt unlucky and did not dare invest more than 20 per cent of my assets in equity, even when the market seemed promising.

Risk taking is abundantly evident in casinos. When people win and feel lucky, they tend to continue gambling and take more risks, believing that they will continue to win. The researchers examined whether hand washing would decrease the effect of previous luck, good or bad, on risk taking. They asked 50 business students to participate in a study. Half of the students were asked to recall a recent incident in which they were lucky financially, such as winning a lottery. The other half were asked to recall an incident in which they were unlucky financially, such as buying several lottery tickets and not winning with any of them. Students described the incidents and their feelings. Following their descriptions, the students were asked to evaluate an antiseptic wipe in another allegedly unrelated product evaluation study. As in the studies on cognitive dissonance, half of the students from each group just examined the wipe without using it, while the other half were asked to use the wipe to clean their hands.

Finally, in the last part of the study, the participants were asked to assume the role of a CEO and to decide whether to improve the company's product. They were told that if they were to reject the decision, profits would remain the same, $20 million a year. If they decided to improve the product, then there was a 75 per cent chance that the profits would rise to $24 million a year but a 25 per cent chance that they would drop to $12 million a year.

Among those who did not clean their hands, the familiar phenomenon emerged once again: those who recalled a good-luck episode took the risk more often than did those who recalled a bad-luck episode. Simply put, the luckier they felt, the more risk they were willing to take. Nothing surprising about that. The interesting part is that the previous experience of good or bad luck did not seem to influence the risk taking of those who cleaned their hands. In short, cleaning the hands eliminated the influence of previous luck, good or bad.

To see if they could replicate these extraordinary results, the researchers conducted an additional study, this time having the participants actually play a game where they could win or lose money and consequently feel lucky or unlucky. As in the first study, they also asked the participants to evaluate an organic soap, with half of the participants simply examining the soap and the other half washing their hands with it. Then the researchers measured how much risk participants were willing to take in a betting game.

The results were consistent with those of the first study. When the participants did not wash their hands, previous luck influenced their risk taking: those who were lucky in the previous round took a greater risk in the next round and bet higher than did those who had been unlucky. For those who had cleaned their hands, however, previous luck was not an influence.

These studies demonstrate that in the short term, the act of washing or cleaning can have a discernible impact on our subsequent behaviours and decisions. It is as if physical cleaning can remove the psychological traces of events in the very recent past so that those events have no influence on our behaviour. While major life occurrences are not easily erased, small daily experiences may be perceived as more malleable, and we may be able to control their influence on our future by physical cleaning.

Our day-to-day experiences influence our decisions, reactions, experiences and emotions in a continuous feedback loop. For example, positive feedback in one event can easily influence performance in the next event, even if the two are unrelated. We all have 'bad days' and 'good days', days we receive good feedback and days we receive bad feedback, days we succeed and days we fail; and our subsequent behaviours and decisions are affected by these experiences. We may perceive the same situation and the same behaviour differently, and may come to different decisions based on previous experiences. Almost all of us, for example, have at some point encountered an ill-disposed waiter or an unfriendly cashier. This unpleasant experience, fresh in our minds, can sour the next encounter we have with an innocent co-worker, friend, or child. Yet if we think back to the first encounter, could our perception of the service provider's behaviour have been influenced by a previous event in our own life or day? Was the waiter or cashier really *that* grouchy?

While most people can never truly wipe the slate clean, so to speak, the aforementioned studies have found that physically cleaning can in fact minimise the effect of prior experience on subsequent behaviour, almost as if the cleaning did wash away some trace of the past. Perhaps with something as simple as washing your face, for example, you can wash away the past and soak in the present.

A simple tactic like washing can be extraordinarily valuable in your daily life. When you find yourself overwhelmed with emotional and cognitive stimuli, struggling to juggle work, family, friends and leisure time, washing your hands might be the perfect way to let go. It may also help you to adjust to the abrupt transitions you make between stress at work and life at home so you do not take your work home with you. Taking a shower often improves our feeling of well-being, and we now have proof that something more is going on than physical cleaning of dirt. Cleaning has the power to eliminate traces of the past; it can refresh and rejuvenate our bodies as well as our focus and concentration on the present moment. These deliberate acts can help us to turn the proverbial page, draw clearer boundaries between the multiple circumstances and activities we juggle, and be truly present in the moment and dedicated to the task at hand.

10

Sweet Smell of Success: Taste and Smell

It Tastes Like Honey

A.A. Milne's universally beloved character Winnie-the-Pooh has delighted generations of children in dozens of languages. Many of Pooh's adventures begin in search of honey, and many of his troubles are the result of his single-minded pursuit of it. Real bears are not quite as steadfastly focused on sweets but are fierce animals that eat meat, among other things. Nevertheless, Milne may have chosen honey as Pooh's obsession to emphasise how sweet-natured his character really is. A friendly bear, Pooh loves company and enjoys helping his friends.

Honey, one of the sweetest foods, is often used to symbolise good and desirable things. During the dinner to celebrate the Jewish New Year, a common tradition is to eat slices of apple dipped in honey as well as honey cake. The sweetness of the honey represents our hope for a felicitous year.

Honey has also been used in certain Orthodox Jewish communities to celebrate the first time a child is brought to school to study the Bible. As part of a ceremony, the rabbi places honey on a slate on which biblical verses are written, and the child licks the honey from the letters. The child also receives a piece of honey cake, with sacred words written on it. It was believed that by licking the sweet honey and eating honey cake, the young child would come to associate Bible studies with sweetness, and studying the Bible would be a pleasurable and satisfying experience.

The association between sweet taste and congenial and pleasant characteristics is beautifully demonstrated in the 2000 film *Chocolat*, starring Juliette Binoche and based on the novel by Joanne Harris. Binoche plays a young woman, Vianne, who travels to a small, conservative French village and opens a *chocolaterie*, much to the displeasure of the severe parish priest who leads the community. Vianne's charming personality and sweet, friendly disposition – as well as her chocolates – soon win over many of the townspeople. People who enter her *chocolaterie* only to have a cup of hot chocolate or to pick up some of her confections quickly develop a warm personal connection with Vianne. She and her daughter bring sweetness to the lives of the townspeople with both their candy and their personal charm.

It is not surprising that we associate sweet taste with good and lovable things. For most of us, sweet tastes are pleasurable. Few are the children who don't love sweets and chocolate, and their parents' job is to control the amount they consume. My three-year-old granddaughter, Natalie, would do anything for sweets, the best tangible reward she can imagine. Most parents know too well the unpleasant experience of passing a sweet shop and having to deny their children's request to buy up half the store.

Most adults also enjoy sweet foods, although many of us would love to be able to control ourselves and eat less of them, being all too aware of the risks that excess sweets pose to our health and figures. Still, we crave sweetness and even demand alternative sweeteners to try to get around the negative effects of eating too much sugar.

This association between sweetness and congeniality is clearly expressed in metaphors and endearments such *a sweet person, sweetie pie, a sweet message, sweetheart* and *a sweet thing to do,* which describe nice people or deeds, congeniality, kindness and thoughtfulness. To sweet-talk is to say flattering things, and sweetness is ultimately what we want to hear. In the Psalms, David describes God's word: 'How sweet are your words to my taste, sweeter than honey to my mouth!' (119:103).

Does the knowledge that a person is fond of sweet things influence what we think of that person? More specifically, do we judge a person who enjoys sweet things as being sweeter? To probe this question, a group of researchers conducted several experiments.[1] In one experiment they presented photos of strangers to 90 students. Each photo was displayed for only a short time with a statement next to it indicating what foods the person in it was fond of. The food item could be bitter (e.g. grapefruit), sour (e.g. lemon), spicy (e.g. peppers), salty (e.g. pretzels), or sweet (e.g. candy). The participants were asked to rate the person in the photo on three attributes: agreeableness, extroversion and neuroticism. Participants rated those who liked sweet foods as more agreeable than those who fancied other foods. There were no differences in the ratings of extroversion or neuroticism; the ratings differed only on agreeableness. Those who said they liked sweet things were perceived to be sweeter people.

The study's findings suggest that when we interact with someone who eats sweet things, we are likely to perceive that person as being nicer, more genial. On occasions such as first dates or business meetings, a person who orders cake or makes a remark about his or her sweet tooth might be perceived as nicer. This judgement of others, based on their predilection for sweets, might affect our own behaviours. For instance, when we believe a person is agreeable, we might be primed to be more cooperative and to compromise. We may judge as better a bid or offer from a person we perceive to be pleasant and agreeable than one from someone we're not predisposed to like.

A more interesting question, to my mind, is whether ingesting sweet tastes actually affects our behaviour. Is it possible that the mere taste of a sweet is enough to trigger more prosocial behaviour? In order to examine this, the researchers divided 55 students into three groups, telling two of the groups they would be tasting a particular food and then asked to comment on it. One group, the sweet-taste group, tasted milk chocolate. The second group, the non-sweet group, tasted an unsweetened cracker containing no sugar at all; and the third group, the no-taste group, was given nothing to taste.

When the experiment was ostensibly over, the participants were told that another professor was looking for volunteers to participate in a separate study but that this professor could not give any compensation in monetary payment or credit hours. Each participant could choose how many minutes, ranging from zero to 30, he or she would like to volunteer. Those who had tasted the milk chocolate volunteered for a greater number of minutes than did those who tasted a non-sweet food or those who tasted nothing. Just tasting sweet milk chocolate made members of the sweet taste group more willing to help someone else. In other words, tasting something sweet made them sweeter, at least in the short term.

I should add that the researchers also checked participants' moods by asking them to complete a questionnaire regarding their positive and negative emotions. They found that the influence of the sweet taste on prosocial and helpful behaviour was not due to positive moods such as the happiness that might result when one eats something sweet. They found that when we eat sweet food, we may behave in a nicer, more prosocial manner and be more willing to help others if necessary.

This information may be quite useful. When arguing with someone, or when you want someone to be nice to you, offer that person a sweet drink, a chocolate bar, or a piece of cake – you may improve the person's behaviour and cause him or her to become more willing to help and avoid conflict. These findings should not be taken to mean that eating sweets will make a huge change in a person's behaviour. They do suggest, however, that there is a correlation between eating sweet food and behaving in a nicer manner.

Sweetness is not the only taste we use metaphorically. Other tastes that describe various behaviours, situations and personalities include these: the party ended on a *sour* note, he stayed to the *bitter* end, he is a *bitter* man, those *spicy* girls. To date, research has focused mainly on the sweet taste, but in my lab we are currently conducting a series of studies on bitter and spicy tastes and various behaviours and judgements related to them. For example, does a bitter taste influence the extent to which individuals tend to complain and be unsatisfied? I hope I will have interesting results to report in the near future.

One Big Mac, Please. No Pickles. No Patience.

Food affects us in ways other than just taste. Apparently, simply being exposed to the logos of some food chains has the power to influence our behaviour. The food industry spends a lot of money on advertising as well as in studying the influence of brand logos and advertisements on consumer behaviour. These studies tend to focus on consumers' buying practices and investigate factors that influence consumers' judgements of products, as well as their shopping intentions and purchasing decisions. However, recent studies have shown that exposure to brand logos affects behaviours that are unrelated to shopping intentions and purchasing. Logos of certain brands actually prompt behaviours that are associated with the brand name or the brand's characteristics. Let's look at one such study from the food industry.

What word or phrase comes to your mind when you think of McDonald's, KFC or Burger King? Most people think of *fast* or *fast food,* and associate that with food prepared quickly, served quickly, and eaten quickly. Numerous studies have investigated the connection between eating fast food, obesity and health problems, and public health campaigns have attempted to raise awareness of the negative consequences of fast food and warn against eating too much of it. The study I'm interested in, however, focuses not on how fast food influences our bodies but rather on how it affects our minds. Fast food symbolises time saved and instant gratification. Is it possible that mere exposure to fast-food logos can influence how fast and impatient we are in domains unrelated to eating?

A group of researchers conducted three experiments to examine this question.[2] In the first experiment, they subliminally exposed half the students in the study to six logo images of fast-food chains, such as McDonald's, Burger King and KFC. These students were asked to focus on the centre of a computer screen while the logos were presented for twelve milliseconds, so short a time that no one could consciously recognise what appeared on the screen. Indeed, the only things all students reported seeing were meaningless colour blocks. The second group, the control group, was exposed to blank squares for the same length of time.

In order to test whether subliminal exposure to fast-food logos would activate a faster mode of behaviour, participants were asked to read a paragraph of 320 words describing the city of Toronto. The students did not know that the time it took them to read the paragraph was recorded. The results clearly showed that those who were exposed to the fast-food logos read the paragraphs faster than did those who were exposed merely to blank squares.

To further investigate the influence of fast food cues, researchers conducted a second experiment. This time they did not present participants with fast-food logos but instead asked one group to recall a time that they went to eat at a fast-food restaurant and the other group to recall a time when they went to a grocery store. Then researchers asked the students to participate in a marketing study (supposedly unrelated to the previous study) and complete a survey in which they were to rate the desirability of several products. There were four pairs of products, each pair pitting a time-saving product against a conventional product: a four-slice toaster versus a single-slice toaster, a two-in-one shampoo and conditioner versus regular shampoo, a high-efficiency detergent versus regular detergent, and a three-in-one skin care product versus a regular skin care product.

The researchers believed that the more impatient people were, the more they would appreciate time-saving products, and indeed, results showed that the memory of a visit to a fast-food restaurant activated the desire for more speed. Those who recalled eating a fast-food meal rated the time-saving products as more desirable than did those who recalled entering a grocery store. Just thinking about fast food made the participants more impatient and led them to want time-saving products.

In a third experiment, the researchers measured the decision to save money. Saving delays gratification. Delayed gratification means putting off the acquisition of something in the present in order to obtain something even better in the future. Parents have to teach this concept to their children, who usually find it difficult not to receive what they want when they want it. Researchers wanted to examine whether simply exposing participants to fast-food cues would influence their saving behaviour, representing their ability to delay gratification.

To that end, the researchers presented 58 students with four logos and asked them to rate the logos' aesthetic qualities. For half of the participants, two of the logos were for fast-food chains, McDonald's and KFC; for the other half, two of the logos were of diners that were inexpensive, but not specifically for fast food. The students were asked to choose between two amounts of money, a smaller sum they could have that day or a bigger one in a week's time. Those who were exposed to the fast-food logos were more willing to accept a smaller sum of money right away. The fast-food-related images influenced their economic decisions. Unless you really need the money immediately, the wiser economic decision would be to wait to receive a bigger sum. The results revealed a relationship between exposure to fast-food logos and poor economic decision making. Just as some of us prefer buying lunch at a fast-food place in order to satisfy our hunger quickly rather than waiting in a restaurant where the food would be better, participants preferred receiving their money immediately rather than waiting for a larger sum later.

These findings suggest that fast food holds much larger sway over us than previously understood. Being exposed to fast-food logos, consciously or unconsciously, or even recalling a visit to McDonald's, might be enough to influence our behaviour in activities unrelated to eating. These results are somewhat frightening. Think of all the times you are exposed to fast-food-chain logos while walking or driving. Is it possible that seeing these logos makes you more impatient and, as a result, causes you to take unnecessary risks when crossing the road, honk more frequently in a traffic jam, or become more impatient with the passengers in your car? Fast food affects how quickly we will try to get things done; this has its merits and advantages in some situations, but being impatient or desiring immediate gratification can spoil your enjoyment of other situations, such as strolling through an art exhibition, reading a book, or just taking in a beautiful view.

Put Yourself on the Scent

Smell has an influence on our emotions, behaviour and judgements. Among the most well-known influences of odours is their effect on consumer behaviour. Estate agents recommend that when you want to sell a house, you bake bread or cookies (vanilla is particularly evocative) in order to favourably influence potential buyers. Several studies have shown that when a pleasant smell is present, people spend more time and more money in stores, and they give more positive evaluations of products. In a study conducted in a big, prestigious clothing store, researchers diffused a pleasant scent for one week and compared the behaviour of customers during that week with customer behaviour during another week, when no scent was diffused.[3] In the presence of a pleasant scent, shoppers evaluated the store and its products more positively and expressed a greater intention to revisit the store.

Another study found that a pleasant ambient smell influenced the amount of money spent – however, only by young shoppers.[4] In yet another study, researchers told participants that a group of students was thinking of establishing a store near the campus that would contain all kinds of items.[5] Students were asked to enter a simulated store and evaluate it and its products. One group of students visited the simulated store while it was scented with lavender, ginger, spearmint, or orange, whereas other students visited the store when it was not scented. In comparison with students who visited the unscented store, those who visited the scented store liked it and its products more.

Marketers are well aware of the influence of smell. Numerous stores, restaurants, clubs and hotels diffuse pleasant scents in their establishments. According to Karen Ravn of the *Los Angeles Times,* when the retailer Verizon introduced the new LG Chocolate phone, it diffused a scent of chocolate in many of its stores.[6] Pleasant ambient smells also affect the behavior and judgements of the clientele in establishments other than stores. A study conducted in a Las Vegas casino found that people gambled to a greater extent on days when the slot machine area of a casino was odorised compared with days when no odour was diffused.[7] In a field study conducted in a pizzeria in a small town in Brittany, researchers found that customers remained longer and spent more money when a lavender scent was diffused in the restaurant.[8] People also danced more in dance clubs and evaluated the evening as more pleasant when a scent of orange, seawater, or peppermint was diffused in the clubs than when there was no added scent.[9]

It might surprise you to learn that certain odours influence not only our behaviour as consumers but also our cognitive and athletic performance. Several studies have shown that peppermint and cinnamon scents improved cognitive performance, including attention and memory; clerical tasks, such as typing speed and alphabetisation; and performance in video games.[10] A peppermint scent also has an effect in the athletic sphere. For example, participants in a study were asked to undergo a fifteen-minute treadmill stress test.[11] Those who performed the task in a peppermint-scented room perceived the task as less difficult. Another study showed that peppermint affects not only perceived difficulty but also athletic performance.[12] Athletes in the peppermint-scented room ran faster, exhibited stronger handgrips, and performed more push-ups than others in a non-scented room.

Next time you have to study for a test, write a paper or report, or pay bills, make your task more enjoyable – and speedy – with the scent of cinnamon or peppermint. Perhaps you could chew gum or a mint, or just open your spice cabinet for a whiff before you begin! Or get yourself a cinnamon- or peppermint-scented air freshener. What a simple, enjoyable trick to use to get through a not-so-enjoyable task.

Several studies have shown that pleasant smells influence our interactions with other people. One of the most liked scents is that of a freshly baked croissant with a fresh cup of coffee on the side. You may like this smell, too, but did you know that it can enhance your interactions with others? In one study, people in a shopping mall were approached at different locations, either near pleasant-smelling establishments such as bakeries and roasted-coffee cafés, or near locations lacking any specific pleasant smell, such as clothing stores.[13] The request was simple: Could the person give change for a dollar bill? A greater number of people changed the dollar bill in the pleasant-smelling locations.

The smell of fresh-baked pastries influences not only helping behaviour but also romantic interactions. In a study conducted in a shopping mall, young men approached young women and asked for their telephone numbers.[14] The potential suitors approached the women in two areas of the mall: areas with pleasant ambient scents, such as near pastry shops and bakeries, or areas near stores with no particular scent. More women gave their phone numbers to the men in the areas with the pleasant smells.

If you're looking to attract the attentions of a stranger, try to do so in a nicely scented room! If you happen to be in a mall, look for the nearest bakery or fresh-brewed coffee establishment and take action there. Based on these findings, your chances are greater in good-smelling food and beverage stores than elsewhere.

Good scents can also help people in awkward situations, such as sitting in a room full of strangers while waiting for a doctor's appointment or an interview, or simply sitting in a hotel lobby while waiting for your room to be ready or for a friend to meet you. Researchers compared the interactions of strangers sitting in a waiting room under two conditions: a scented and an unscented room.[15] Those who sat in a room scented with geranium essence oil exhibited more interactions with other people in the room. There were more social interactions – such as conversations, eye contact and physical contact – and there was a shorter physical distance between people: they sat in chairs closer together rather than taking the seats farther away from others.

Pleasant smells positively influence our moods and consequently enhance our interactions with others, our willingness to help them, and our tendency to evaluate places such as stores and restaurants as more pleasant. But sometimes a smell activates concepts that are somatically related to that specific smell. For example, a scent of cleaning product activates the mental association with cleaning and consequently a cleaning-related behaviour. Researchers showed participants several letter sequences and asked them to indicate as rapidly as possible whether they saw a word (e.g. *different*) or a non-word (e.g. *rinexe*).[16] Some of the words were cleaning-related, such as *hygiene* or *tidying*, while others were not related to cleaning: *computer* or *bicycling*, for example. Half of the participants were seated in a room scented with the citrus odour of a cleaning product, while the other half were assigned the task in a room with no scent. Those who sat in the scented room reacted faster to the cleaning-related words than did those who sat in the unscented room. Participants were unaware that the cleaning scents influenced their performance.

In a second experiment, the researchers asked participants who were sitting either in a room with a clean (citrus) scent or in an unscented room to list five activities they were planning to do that day. Those who sat in the scented room wrote down a greater number of cleaning-related activities than did those who sat in the unscented room.

A third experiment, however, was the most interesting. Again the researchers had participants sitting in either a clean-scented or an unscented room, but this time they asked the participants to respond to a questionnaire. Yet the questionnaire was actually irrelevant to the study; its only purpose was to seat the participants in either the scented or the unscented room. After filling out the questionnaire, all the participants were moved to another, unscented room and asked to eat a biscuit that produced a lot of crumbs. A hidden camera recorded the participants, enabling the researchers to examine participants' behaviour later. Those participants who had sat in a room with a cleaning-related scent cleaned the crumbs off the table more often than did those who had sat in the unscented room.

It's quite amazing. Simply smelling a cleaning-related scent influences our cleaning behaviour. Want your child, spouse, or roommate to clean his or her room or the apartment? Just scatter around some cleaning-related substances to scent up the room. These experimental findings suggest that there is a greater chance the person will be motivated to clean up.

This study demonstrated that a certain smell activates a somatically related concept (clean smell activates clean behaviour). By now you can guess that the interesting question for us scientists who study embodiment would be to examine whether smelling a particular odour that is metaphorically linked to a specific behaviour would influence our judgements or behaviour in a similar direction. We saw in Chapter 9 that, according to metaphors such as *clean conscience, rotten apple* and *rotten to the core*, pleasant and disgusting smells were related to moral judgements, and the same moral dilemmas were judged differently according to the ambient smell

When Something Smells Fishy: Scent of Suspicion

Numerous metaphors, such as *something smells fishy* and *that idea stinks*, use smell to describe bad things. *I can smell something is up* recruits smell in its capacity as a detector. Two researchers conducted a pair of studies in which they tested the common metaphor *something smells fishy,* which implies that we have a suspicion something is wrong – to see whether an actual fishy smell would trigger people's suspicions.[17] Both studies used games to examine suspicious behaviour, though not games like Monopoly or basketball but rather a carefully designed task-oriented setup called the Trust Game that seeks to elicit specific behaviours from subjects in a controlled environment. This game has strict rules and enables researchers to examine various behaviours, such as trust, generosity and egocentrism. This method is better than directly questioning participants about their various behaviours and is easier than watching them in real-life situations, which contain too many variables to control.

The researchers asked 45 students to participate in an investment decision project, which was really an exercise in trust. Each participant went to the laboratory with another 'participant', who was actually part of the experiment. Each of the two received twenty quarters. There were two roles in this game: the sender decided how much money to send to the receiver. The money sent was quadrupled, and the receiver decided how much money to return to the sender. The more the sender trusted the receiver and believed the receiver would be fair and return more money, the more money the sender would send.

For example, if the sender sent ten quarters out of the twenty, they immediately became forty. If the receiver was fair and sent back half, then the sender would get twenty quarters, double what he or she originally sent. On the other hand, if the receiver returned only five quarters, the sender lost money. Since the purpose of the study was to investigate suspicion and not fairness, the real participants were invariably assigned the role of the sender. They were told that at the end of the game they would take the money home.

Participants were divided into three groups, and each group's play-ing area was sprayed with a different scent. One group smelled fish oil, one smelled fart spray, and the third group's area was sprayed with odourless tap water. The researchers chose to use the fart spray for one group because they wanted to examine whether *any* unpleas-ant smell might influence suspicion or whether the influencing factor is specifically the fishy smell (the one that is metaphorically related to suspicion). The researchers found that indeed, participants who were exposed to the fishy smell sent less money than those who were exposed to no odour or to the fart spray. Not one of the participants was able to guess the purpose of the study.

The second study also examined suspicion, this time using a game called the Public Goods Game. In this game, each participant received twenty quarters with the option of investing as much as he or she chose into a common pool. Each was told that the money invested would be multiplied and subsequently divided equally among the par-ticipants – regardless of the amount of money each invested – and would be theirs to take home. Since the money was multiplied, if all participants invested more money, then everybody should take home more money.

A suspicious player would tend to believe that others were not putting as much as she was into the common pool; and since the money was equally divided, she would not want to be the sucker putting in more money than others. Consequently a distrustful per-son would put in less money. A trusting person would not suspect the other participants and would put more into the common pool. In other words, the more suspicious one is of others' intentions, the less money she would put into the pool. As in the first study, partici-pants were divided into three groups and three odours were sprayed in the areas where the experiment was conducted. Again, those who were exposed to a fishy smell invested less money in the common pool than did those who were exposed to fart spray or the odourless water spray.

Taken together, these two studies demonstrate that the mere smelling of a fishy odour was enough to make people suspicious. Without being aware of it, the participants were influenced by the metaphorical link between a fishy smell and suspicion. The sensory experience affected the abstract concept and subsequently the psychological judgement and behaviour.

The researchers then wanted to study whether the link between fish odour and suspicion exists in reverse. In other words, would those who are more suspicious be more likely to detect a fishy smell? To examine this hypothesis, the researchers invited 80 students to the laboratory and divided them into two groups, a suspicious group and a non-suspicious group. Both groups were asked to smell five odours and to identify the smells in writing. One of the smells was of fish oil, and the four others were orange nectar, minced onion, autumn apple fragrance oil and creamy caramel.

In the non-suspicious group, participants were simply asked to sniff each tube and write down the smell. For the other group, the experimenter created a suspicious atmosphere by behaving as if she was hiding something: for instance, she would suddenly take a document that was placed underneath the participants' response sheets, put it in her bag, and smile strangely.

Participants in the suspicious environment were more likely to correctly identify the fish oil. Suspicion did not influence the identification of any of the other smells. The researchers replicated this study with other smells and obtained the same results. Taken together, the experiments indicate that the metaphorical link between a fishy smell and suspicion works both ways. We are more suspicious when we smell fish oil, and we are more inclined to detect the smell of fish oil when we are suspicious.

Once again, we have clear evidence that we think metaphorically. We associate fishy smells and suspicion, and each component of that association activates the other. If you find yourself suddenly wary of a place or a person, or uncomfortable in a situation where more seems to be going on than you can rationally put into words, it may be that your sense of smell is alerting you that something is amiss. Take this information from your ancient olfactory sense seriously and re-evaluate whether you should put your trust in someone when something smells 'off'.

Turning on Lights Outside the Box: Embodying Metaphors

The many revealing studies described in this book have dealt with ways in which our behaviour is influenced by physical sensations that are metaphorically linked to abstract concepts. Some studies manipulated physical sensations such as warmth or cleanliness to examine whether they activate abstract concepts such as friendliness or moral behaviour. Others used abstract concepts to examine whether they influence physical sensations.

But there is another way to investigate the association between metaphors and behaviour: by actually embodying the meanings of the metaphors. Embodying metaphors means acting them out. For example, to embody the metaphor *fishing for information,* one would hold a fishing rod while sitting next to a small pond and actually try to fish for something.

In this chapter, we will see how embodying metaphors influences our emotions and our performance.

Sealing That Bad Feeling

Many rituals and superstitions are actually embodiments of our thoughts and wishes. In a tradition called Tashlikh, which is Hebrew for 'casting off', observant Jews symbolically cast off their sins of the previous year into a vast body of water, such as a lake or sea, in preparation for the new year. To do this, they put pieces of bread or other food, symbolising the sins, in their pockets and then throw the food into the water. As the pieces are carried away by the flowing water, so are the sins.

Another example is the ancient Middle Eastern ritual of guarding against the evil eye. The performer of the ritual must heat a chunk of lead and throw it into a container of water, where it supposedly takes the shape of the evil eye, and then bury it or throw it into the sea. In another ritual, believers write on a piece of paper the name of a person who is troubling them and then throw it out of the house, saying: 'Get out of my life!' This physical throwing out of something that symbolises what we want to be rid of is the very essence of embodiment.

Metaphors such as *I kept my emotions inside, hide your emotions, I buried my feelings* and *I bottled up my anger* treat emotions almost as tangible objects you can control by putting them in a container or using some other physical restraint. A group of researchers wanted to investigate whether embodying these metaphors would actually help keep the emotions inside and allow the individual to feel better.[1]

For their first experiment, the researchers divided students into two groups and asked all of them to write about a decision they regretted. Participants in one group were asked to place the note in an envelope and hand it to the experimenter, while those in the other group were simply asked to hand over what they'd written. Participants from both groups were then asked to indicate their feelings about the event they had just written about, choosing from five negative emotions – guilt, sadness, worry, regret and shame. The students were asked to indicate on a five-point scale to what extent they felt each of these feelings, ranging from not at all to extremely. Those who sealed their recollections of the regrettable events in envelopes felt less negatively about them than did those who simply handed back their answers.

In a second study to examine whether this effect also applies to other events that arouse negative feelings, the researchers asked students to write about something they strongly desired but did not get. Again, half of the students were asked to put their written stories in envelopes whereas the other half were simply asked to hand over their pages. All were then asked to indicate how they felt about their remembered events, using four emotions: sadness, disappointment, anxiety and dissatisfaction. As in the first study, those who put their answers in envelopes felt less negatively about their events than did those who did not put their stories in envelopes.

Just embodying the metaphor by putting their writing in an envelope was enough to make the participants feel better. This result suggests that when we are upset about something, writing down what happened, sealing it, and putting it in a drawer, or even throwing it away, might ease our feelings, at least temporarily. Evidence suggests that keeping a secret is burdensome, but writing about it in a diary, for example, could ease that burden. This study suggests that sealing what we write might ease negative feelings associated with the secret.

On New Year's Eve, our tradition is to make personal resolutions. People will promise, for example, to lose weight, to behave better, or to make more of an effort to achieve a goal. I have friends who put a twist on that tradition. Every year, they throw a New Year's Eve party at their country house and build a big bonfire. They pass out paper and pens and ask their guests to write down any negative things about the past year – regrets, frustrations, disappointments. The guests then throw their papers into the fire and watch them burn away. This is cathartic. Expressing yourself, getting your deepest feelings out of your head and watching them disappear, will help you move on. My friends believe that doing this is infinitely more helpful than simply making promises – or talking about making promises – which may never be kept.

Many of us have done things we have come to regret or lamented not getting things we wanted. More often than not, the regret is not debilitating and life goes on. If you're unable to get over something, however, try to write about it and then put your writing in an envelope in a drawer, or simply throw it away. It might help, and it is definitely cheaper than a therapist.

Embodying Creative Metaphors

I am a great believer in the value of creative thinking, and I admire and respect creative people. For elementary and middle school, my two sons were educated at a school for the arts, where they had many hours of painting and sculpture instruction and were exposed to music, drama and dancing more than the average child. My son Dani was a great painter and wrote beautiful poems. My son Dory is a professional musician, a performer and a writer. My daughter, Orly, who is a law professor, has already written several books and channels her creative thinking into her research on intellectual property and innovation. My husband, David, is a medical doctor as well as a painter, a sculptor and the inventor of several medical gadgets. My brother, Raffi, was a successful fashion designer in Israel and the United States and is now well known for his glass designs. I am happy to be surrounded by creative people.

Creative people influence and shape our lives. So many inventions – like the telephone, electrical power, the Internet, the smartphone and Facebook – are now taken for granted. They changed our lives so radically that we can't imagine living without them. Although some people are more naturally creative than others, there is a lot we can do to enhance our creativity. Most of us will not write great music like Mozart or a classic book like *The Catcher in the Rye*, or invent the next Velcro, paper clip, or breakfast cereal and change many lives, but we can still be creative in our daily lives and in our jobs. Several studies have demonstrated that relatively simple actions and gestures can enhance our creative thinking.

My father used to tell an old joke about a man who showed up at the Ministry of Defence saying he had an original idea to build an aeroplane that would fly from one country to the other without a pilot, and the passengers would be served by a robot. 'That is a great idea,' he was told, 'but how are you going to do it?' 'Sorry,' he said, 'I only have the idea.' How often does that happen? A person will come up with a novel idea but be unable to devise the subsequent creative ideas to develop it.

We describe creative thinking with metaphors such as *thinking outside the box, putting two and two together* and *on the one hand … and on the other hand*, which suggest that we have to think about a problem from various angles and perspectives, and be flexible and unconventional, in order to avoid stagnant thinking and behaviour. These are all characteristics of creative thinking. In order to be creative and arrive at new ideas, we have to think differently, see several sides of the issue, and be flexible enough to combine ideas that seem only tangentially related. Sometimes we have all the information but still can't see the solution.

I'm going to show you that just by embodying certain metaphors, by working with your body or imagining certain body movements, you can become more creative. In fact, even exposure to creative cues in the environment is enough to enhance your creativity.

On the One Hand ... and On the Other Hand

There is often more than one side to a problem and more than one
perspective from which to view a situation. Indeed, creative ideas
often come when we think of a problem from another point of view. A
group of researchers conducted several studies that examined whether
embodying various metaphors related to creativity will increase creativity.[2] In the first study they examined the metaphor *on the one hand
... and on the other hand*. Specifically, they wanted to investigate if
just asking participants to raise one hand and then the other would
increase their creativity.

The researchers asked 40 students to participate in two ostensibly
unrelated studies that were conducted simultaneously. Participants
were asked to think about new ideas for a university building complex
and, while doing so, to take part in a public speaking study in which
they were to raise one arm and stretch it up, approximating a gesture
typically made by public speakers.

The study was conducted in two parts. In the first part, all students
were holding their right hands up towards the wall and their left hands
behind their backs while giving various ideas for uses for the university
building. In the second part of the study, all students were asked to
think about more ideas for the building's use and say them loudly.
Half of the students were asked again to raise their right hands, but
the other half were asked to switch hands and hold their left hands
towards the wall and their right hands behind their backs.

The students' answers were audio-recorded, and two raters – who
had no idea what hand each participant raised – coded their creativity
according to two criteria: the number of ideas participants had and
the number of unique answers they gave.

The results are amazing. Participants who switched hands in the
second part of the study offered more ideas, and their ideas were

coded as more original and flexible. In short, they were more creative. These differences were not found in the first part of the study, in
which all participants raised their right hands.

Don't Box Yourself In

Thinking outside the box is generally understood to mean being creative and flexible, not sticking to conventions but looking at a problem
from a new perspective in order to come up with novel ideas.

The same researchers wanted to examine whether the embodiment
of the metaphor *thinking outside the box* would influence creativity.
They presented 102 students with items from a test called the Remote
Associates Test, which is designed to measure creativity.[3] In it, the test
taker reads groups of three words and has to find a word that relates
to each of the three. For example: *falling, actor, dust* – the answer is
star. Another example: *opera, hands, dishes* – the answer is *soap*. One
needs to think creatively to find such remote relationships. In short,
one needs to think outside the box.

For the study, the researchers constructed a box five feet square
and divided participants into three groups. One group took the test
sitting inside the box, the second group took the test sitting outside
the box, and the third group completed the test with no box in the
room. Those who completed the test outside the box correctly solved
more problems than those who sat inside the box or those who sat
in a room with no box. Embodying the metaphor *thinking outside
the box* influenced how creative they were. The researchers ruled out
the possibility that sitting inside the box was not comfortable or that
it aroused anxiety in claustrophobic individuals. They found that the
differences between the groups were not due to differences in the
feelings related to sitting inside and outside the box.

The researchers conducted another study, in which all participants

were shown pictures of objects made of Lego blocks and asked to
think of various objects that these pictures could represent. This time,
however, instead of putting participants inside or outside a box, the
researchers manipulated their freedom to move about. Participants
in one group were asked to consider the task while walking along a
fixed rectangular path indicated by a trail of duct tape on the floor,
whereas those in the other group were told to walk freely around the
room. The results showed clearly that participants who walked freely
generated more original ideas.

In a third study the researchers investigated whether simple mental
representations of body movement would be sufficient to enhance
creative thinking. In other words, could just imagining walking along
a fixed path or moving freely influence creativity? Participants were
asked to move an avatar and to imagine that they were the avatar in
another life. As participants walked their avatars, they were to think
of as many ideas as possible for creative gifts they would give to an
acquaintance. One group walked the avatar along a fixed path, and
the other group walked the avatar freely. Those who walked the avatar
freely generated more original ideas (for example, a magazine sub-
scription) than did those who walked the avatar along a fixed path
(whose ideas included, for example, a CD).

These striking results suggest that embodying the metaphor *outside the box* enhances creativity. They further suggest that you do not
have to sit outside a box; you can walk freely in the room rather than
along a fixed path or even imagine that you are walking freely in the
room to think more creatively.

Putting Two and Two Together: It Does Add Up!

Sometimes, in order to solve a problem, we only need to look at what
we have and use the information in front of us: in other words, 'put

two and two together'. In order to use the information at our disposal, however, we sometimes have to think unconventionally.

To examine whether embodiment of the metaphor *putting two and two together* would increase creativity, the researchers cut paper coasters into halves and divided participants into two groups. For one group, the coaster halves were put in two piles: one on the left side of the table and the other on the right. Participants were asked to simultaneously remove one half from the left and another half from the right and combine the two halves in the middle of the table. Participants in the other group were given only one pile of coaster halves and asked to transfer them into the middle. In this way, one group really put two things together while the other just moved things from one place to the other.

Participants were then given the Remote Associates Test. Those who moved the two halves simultaneously and combined them to make a whole solved more questions than those who moved only one pile. Simply embodying the idea of putting two and two together increased their creativity.

Walking freely around the room or outside helps to free you from conventions and barriers and allows you to think in a different, creative way. When you alternate gestures with your hands, you help yourself think of new ideas, and when you physically combine things, you help yourself see remote associations. Sometimes, even imagining yourself walking freely – not only physical embodiment but also mental embodiment – is sufficient to increase creativity. In all these studies the researchers did not explicitly refer to a metaphor. Participants embodied the meaning of the metaphor but did not hear it or speak of it.

These results have significant implications. Creative thinking is crucial in many disciplines, and all professionals can be better served by creative thinking. Painters, musicians, writers, animators, designers, architects, inventors, scientists, high-tech programmers and doctors need to think creatively. Teachers must constantly think creatively about how to make their classes interesting. Politicians and policy makers need to find creative solutions to our complicated social problems. Many tasks in our everyday lives have no straightforward answers. We parents have to be creative when we try to juggle childcare duties with career responsibilities. We want to educate our children in a positive way, to be understanding and yet to draw boundaries. Creativity is important in cooking, not only to concoct tasty, healthy dishes that will appeal to our families but also to use up foods that would otherwise spoil.

New ideas will also help improve our relationships with our spouses when neither arguing nor polite requests work. How can I stop my spouse from putting his papers, bag and everything else on the dining room table? Perhaps I could offer him a tangible reward for stowing them in another designated area, or I could arrange the table in such a way that it will be impossible to put anything on it, or I could find another small table near the door that would be for his stuff alone.

With practice, you can learn to be creative and use creativity to enhance your work and home environments. Try alternating the hand you work with; use simple gestures and movements like those the psychologists asked the participants in their studies to make. See if you can find solutions to everyday problems and challenges. How can we arrange our clothes in such a way that they don't wrinkle and we can find them easily? How do we keep our desks tidy and our e-mail orderly? I myself am still looking for this particular creative idea.

People in creative occupations like advertising, animation, high tech and media should think carefully about the work environment. Boring, constrained environments stifle creativity. Encourage freedom of movement in your workplace; open up work spaces so they don't resemble boxes or cubicles.

The structured environment of many schools may be limiting children's capacity for creative thinking by placing a higher premium on logic, facts and conformity. 'I have never let my schooling interfere with my education,' said Mark Twain. Indeed, many schools still subscribe to the traditional model of learning while sitting at a desk. Although there is value in teaching children to sit down, focus and work, this model as an overall approach to learning is outdated. Some schools make the learning experience fun and provide 'alternative' areas of learning. For example, at the Ein Hayam Experimental School in Israel, I was particularly struck by how much time students spend outdoors, in the schoolyard, in the small grove adjacent to the school, or at the beach. Children learn by playing games, and teachers believe that their students learn more when they are enjoying themselves. Yet most Western cultures immediately suspect any connection between enjoyment and learning.

The more children enjoy studying, the more they will learn. However, I believe that there is another factor involved: the fact that the children are constantly moving and exposed to so many stimuli and cues in the environment enhances their creative thinking. Learning through play is enjoyable, and the children move around rather than sit in their chairs. They gesture more and expand their physical space.

The importance of physical exercises for learning and creativity has been documented by Harvard professor John Ratey in his book *Spark!*[4] According to Ratey, moving and learning go together. The body and the mind are connected, and physical exercises make the brain function at its best. Children who move and exercise do better on many cognitive tests. In addition, while playing outside, the children are exposed to many stimuli and physical experiences, such as sand between their toes, water on their faces, the smell of flowers, the sounds of birds, trees, and a variety of textures and colours. I suggest that these bodily and sensory motor experiences also enhance creativity and help children grasp abstract concepts.

By that I do not mean to say that we should abolish classrooms and teach school only in the great outdoors. I do suggest, however, that more movement is needed – more field trips, and more time outside the classroom. Beethoven, after finishing his Sixth Symphony, also known as the 'Pastoral', wrote: 'How happy I am to be able to walk among the shrubs, the trees, the woods, the grass, and the rocks! For the woods, the trees, and the rocks give man the resonance he needs.' His walks through Vienna's countryside are said to have inspired that great masterpiece.

If children can learn to trigger their creativity, they are likely to be able to solve problems more readily throughout their lives. This is also true for adults. Get up from time to time and walk around the room. Or better yet, take a walk outside. You won't solve every problem, but you'll increase your chances of reaching more creative solutions.

In the beginning of this book, I told you about my days in the Israeli army, where I served in a bunker with fluorescent lights, not knowing if it was day or night and always breathing the same recycled air. That environment was in sharp contrast to creative schools and workplaces of today. I recently had the opportunity to see photos of the Google offices, which are the opposite of a traditional office, a room furnished with desks and chairs. On the Google 'campus', many workers ride between offices on scooters. The offices themselves have many rooms in which people can relax: rooms that look like comfortable living rooms with televisions and beautiful views where workers can sit and drink cappuccino; games rooms with ping-pong tables, plants and chaises longues; and of course the famous playground slides, where the workers can take a 'recess' break and feel like kids for a few seconds.

These facilities were not put in place just to please the workers. Google knows that the environment has an impact on the human mind, on creativity, and on productivity. It is great, of course, to work in such a beautiful place, but the fact that the employees are moving around and occupying such an interesting space has no doubt contributed to many of the groundbreaking innovations that have made Google so successful.

Shedding Light on a Problem

Have you ever struggled to think of a word in a crossword puzzle? Then suddenly you have an insight and the answer appears. This instance of sudden discovery and realisation is called the *aha experience* or the *eureka effect,* and is attributed to Archimedes, the great Greek mathematician. Archimedes was asked by the king to determine whether his crown was pure gold or whether a dishonest worker had put some silver in it. While Archimedes was pondering the problem in the bath, he realised that the level of the water had risen when he got into the water. He then understood that he could measure the volume of the crown in a similar way, which would help him determine its purity. So excited was Archimedes by his discovery that he ran naked in the streets, shouting 'Eureka!' – Greek for 'I've found it!'

This insight or aha experience is metaphorically related to light. We use metaphors such as *I saw the light* and *shed light on a situation.* The light bulb is often used as a symbol of invention and innovation, and to represent a sudden flash of insight into how to solve a problem. Drawings, cartoons and comic strips depicting new ideas often feature light bulbs over people's heads.

A group of researchers investigated whether people exposed to a light bulb perform better in tasks that require insight and creativity.[5] They conducted a series of studies where they presented participants with problems that required insight while exposing half of them to a light bulb.

In one study, the researchers gave 79 students a problem that required out-of-the-box thinking – to connect four dots arranged in a square with three lines without raising the pencil.

People often find this problem difficult because they assume that there is a boundary around the dots, and therefore they draw the line within the area of the dots. Once they realise that they can draw lines outside the boundary of the dots, they solve the problem easily.

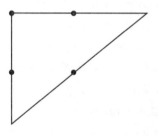

After assigning the dots task, the experimenter mentioned that it was somewhat dark in the room and turned on an incandescent light bulb for half of the participants. For the other half he turned on an overhead fluorescent light. The results are amazing. Forty-four per cent of those who were exposed to a light bulb solved the problem, while only 22 per cent of those who were exposed to the fluorescent lighting solved it. Just being exposed to the incandescent light bulb increased participants' ability to realise that they could go outside the boundary. Similar results were found in a second study when the participants received mathematical questions that required insight. Those who saw an illuminated light bulb solved the mathematical problems more often than those exposed to fluorescent light.

In a third study the researchers gave the participants a creative verbal task, the aforementioned Remote Associates Test, in which participants are presented with three words and have to find a word related to each of the three. For example: what is the word that is related to *widow, bite* and *monkey*? (Answer: *spider.*) Again, the experimenter turned on an incandescent light bulb for one group and an overhead fluorescent light for the other group. The results were consistent. Those who were exposed to the light bulb solved more questions correctly.

The researchers conducted a fourth study in which they once again presented the participants with the Remote Associates Test. However, instead of comparing a bare light bulb with fluorescent light, this time they exposed one group to a bare, illuminated 25-watt bulb. Instead of exposing the other group to an overhead fluorescent light, the researchers exposed them to a shaded 40-watt bulb, using a brighter bulb for the shaded light so that the ambient light would be the same. They once again administered the RAT, and those who saw the bare illuminated light bulb performed better and found more correct words than those who were exposed to the shaded bulb. These results confirm that what enhances creativity is the exposure to the bare illuminated light bulb, which is metaphorically related to innovation and insight and symbolises discovery. Light influences our cognitive processes and leads to greater insight and creative thinking.

An Apple a Day ... Keeps You More Creative

Exposing yourself to symbols associated with insight and creativity can enhance creativity. Even a brand name associated with creativity will increase creative thinking. A group of researchers chose two brands, IBM and Apple.[6] Both are respectable brands, but Apple is more readily associated with creativity than IBM. Moreover, Apple emphasises innovation and non-conformity in its advertisements and uses slogans such as *Think different*. A young friend of mine who has just moved to Apple from another high-tech company told me that although he liked working in the other company, he really felt the creativity in the air at Apple.

Researchers asked a group of students to indicate the extent to which each of these two brands represents various traits, creativity among them. The results clearly showed that Apple was perceived as more creative than IBM. The students were also asked how much they liked each of these brands and how they felt about them. No difference was found regarding these questions. They liked both brands equally and perceived them positively. The only difference was that Apple was perceived as more creative.

The researchers then conducted an experiment with two other groups of participants, who were presented with one number on the computer screen at a time, and whose task was to add the numbers as they appeared. During the presentation of each number, the participants in one group were subliminally exposed to IBM logos and the participants in the other group were subliminally exposed to Apple logos. The logos were presented for a very short time, thirteen milliseconds, too short for participants to consciously recognise the stimuli. Indeed, when participants were asked at the end of the experiment to report what they saw, no one had been aware of seeing any of the logos.

Participants were then given a creativity assignment, the 'unusual uses' task. In this task participants are asked to write as many unusual uses for a brick as they can think of. Possible uses are as a paperweight, a doorstop, or, wrapped in foil, an inexpensive bacon or sandwich press for your grill. The idea behind this task is that the more creative you are, the more you see a brick as having many uses. Those who were subliminally exposed to the Apple logos found more unusual uses for the brick. In addition, two judges evaluated the creativity of the first three uses suggested by each participant. Those who were subliminally exposed to the Apple logos suggested more creative uses. Just subliminal exposure to Apple logos was enough to enhance creativity. Amazing!

To take advantage of these results in your own home or company, consider hanging posters with creativity-related cues, such as drawings of light bulbs or other symbols of creativity: logos or mottoes of other creative companies, a picture of an open field or another setting without boundaries, a room with a very high ceiling, or a person actually sitting or standing outside a box. A print of a Cubist painting by Picasso could also be helpful, since Cubism epitomises different ways of portraying and presenting more than one view at a time. Photos of faraway locations might also boost creativity, since it has been found that travelling abroad increased students' creativity.[7] Have such a poster in your study or above your desk and in your children's rooms. According to these studies, it may help more than you think. Be creative – and think of other symbols that will increase your creativity.

Conclusion

Many studies described in the book have shown that our physical sensations activate abstract concepts and, as a result, influence our behaviours, emotions and thoughts. For example, when we touch a soft object, the sensation influences how gently we will behave. Eating sweet food actually makes us act sweeter. These are remarkable findings.

The studies described in this chapter, however, go one step further. Embodying certain metaphors for creativity or being exposed to creativity-related cues in the environment activates our existing knowledge as well as the ability to be creative, to think of new and original ideas, and to make remote associations. Embodiment of metaphors actually enlarges knowledge and influences performance. The act of embodying the metaphors or being exposed to the creativity-related environmental cues influences your ability to solve problems in ways you might otherwise not have thought of. This is fabulous news. Your creative ability lies squarely in your own hands. Your body can help your mind embody great and small achievements.

Epilogue

As I was writing the final chapter of this book, I heard on the news that an enormous meteorite had exploded over Russia, injuring hundreds of people. This is a strange and rare event. Other natural disasters, such as earthquakes and tsunamis, happen relatively rarely, but the meteorite made me think about how the forces of nature can change people's lives in an instant, with no warning.

This book, however, has not dealt with the obvious, powerful natural forces in the earth, sea and sky that can change our lives in the most dramatic ways. My goal in this book was to focus on the subtler environmental factors that we experience every day but do not notice, although they nonetheless affect our lives significantly. The cutting-edge, innovative studies I've presented demonstrate again and again the surprising effects of various physical sensations, such as tactile perceptions, flavours, weight, colours, vertical positioning and physical cleanliness, on our behaviours, emotions and judgements.

Psychologists and philosophers have known for years that our bodily sensations affect our behaviour, but only in the past few decades has extensive research in embodied cognition systematically examined this interaction and established these amazing connections, showing the metaphorical to be quite physical.

According to embodied cognition theory, we understand abstract concepts via the bodily experiences associated with these concepts. Children learn about the world through their physical sensations and so develop concrete ideas of distance, tactile sensations, warmth, weight and vertical position. For instance, children feel warmth when their parents hold and embrace them and so experience the connection between physical and emotional warmth. They learn the difference between near and far, light and dark, positive and negative, when they are put to bed and their parents leave the room and turn off the light. They learn the connection between height and power when they look up at the grown-ups around them.

These physical sensations constitute the basis and indeed the scaffolding for representing and understanding abstract higher concepts, such as friendliness, emotional distance and status. Our emotions, thoughts and behaviours are grounded in physical sensations. We actually shift our attention upward when we think of powerful people or groups, and believe that an issue is more important when we are carrying something heavy.

Not only are our sensory and motor perceptions, or physical intelligence, important in understanding how our thoughts and emotions work, but they're also vital to building artificial intelligence. As Hans Moravec, an influential robotics inventor, theorist and professor at Carnegie-Mellon University, has said, it is simpler to program a computer to play chess than to program the computer to imitate the perception of a baby. His theory, Moravec's paradox, maintains that in designing robots and developing artificial intelligence, sensorimotor skills require much more computation than high-order cognitive processes, such as decisions or reasoning. Moravec's paradox reminds us that our senses are a miracle and that they connect our intelligence to the world – they even have a role in creating our intelligence.

These studies demonstrate that metaphors are the ideal ambassadors of embodied cognition. Metaphors are all around us, in our speech and thoughts, yet operating invisibly. A metaphor associates a concrete concept with an abstract concept; it makes it easier for us to understand the abstract concept through an immediately comprehensible comparison. We know that a person who is *cold as stone* hasn't actually been standing in the frigid outdoors. A *social climber* doesn't go to ladder parties. And an *emotionally distant* person can actually be sitting quite close to us. Nonetheless, an actual link exists between abstract ideas and our felt sense of the world. This physical intelligence provides valuable information, but it can also make us biased: we are more prone to judge a person as being *cold as stone* when we actually sense cold temperature, even though that assessment may be unfair. Knowing the fluid communication between body and mind can help you guard against making inaccurate judgements and can also help you avoid being taken in by false embodied intelligence.

Some psychologists believe that metaphors are mere reflections of these associations between physical sensations and abstract concepts, but many scientists have found that metaphors are actually part of the process and play an important role in our understanding of abstract concepts. The research described in this book demonstrates that metaphors are more than just figures of speech that enrich and add depth and meaning to our language. In fact, we think metaphorically. Metaphors have evolved to become universal and picturesque units of meaning in our minds. Metaphors are more powerful than we might have imagined and actively influence our thoughts and behaviour.

We have seen cups of hot coffee melt hearts and change opinions, clipboards add heft to the value of currencies, and freshly washed hands provide the licence to cheat. Although you no doubt have felt how outdoor temperature affects your mood, I am sure that you would not have guessed that just touching a warm object can influence your judgement of another person or make you more sociable. Tactile sensations play a much larger role in our lives than we might have believed. You probably never thought that the mere softness of the chair you are sitting on might affect your negotiating style and hence your performance. You may have intuited that gesturing and moving around could help you work out a problem, but you probably never dreamed that actually sitting 'outside the box' improves and enhances your creative thinking.

In describing these experiments and their alluring findings, I occasionally encounter sceptics who say something like 'Well, yes, that study is very interesting, but come on, aren't you stretching things a bit?' It's hard not to believe that something else, something you're missing – an external variable, the experimental design – is causing these outcomes. How can physical sensations that are metaphorically related to emotions and behaviours have such power?

The astonishing findings that I cite in *Sensation* have been conducted by top scientists from leading universities and published in responsible and prestigious scientific journals, with their methodology examined by other scientists. The experiments were carefully designed and controlled, and they randomly assigned participants from the same populations to different groups. There were no other differences between the groups besides the influence that was examined. The experiments were designed to ensure that the manipulation of the examined variables was responsible for the behaviour of the participants.

Nevertheless, whenever scientists hear about findings that are strongly counter-intuitive, their antennae should go up and they should be sceptical. Sometimes astonishing findings do in fact point to badly structured experiments or data that have been manipulated or possibly fabricated. Indeed, there have been a couple of bad apples in embodied cognition research (as well as in other scientific fields) whose findings have been found unreliable due to questionable data. Their papers were retracted, and two of them resigned their university positions. I don't include these discredited psychologists' work, of course, and I myself have also carefully reviewed all the studies that I include in this book, to ensure that I present you with only the most credible, well-developed studies and findings in this exciting new field.

Recently, however, some of the most famous, most cited studies in social psychology have come under attack due to failed attempts to replicate their findings. Most of the studies criticised were not directly related to embodied cognition, the focus of *Sensation*, although some embodied cognition studies were criticised as well. In order to try to ensure that the effects of the studies I use are real, I've mostly cited studies that use multiple experiments, not just one. When several experiments examine the same question using different methods, we can be more certain of their general conclusion, and we have a smaller chance of arriving at an incidental, anomalous finding. In many of the cases I recount, different studies were conducted in different laboratories and sometimes even in different countries, all with similar results. For example, the influence of physical weight on the conception of importance was found in a number of studies conducted in several laboratories, both in the United States and in the Netherlands.

The possibility remains that some of these findings will fail to be replicated. I believe that in the case of embodied cognition studies, the main reason for such a failure is the existence of variable factors, such as surroundings, personality and culture, that were not taken into account. These factors can influence results, and frankly they're not easy to adjust for. Nonetheless, this is a new and exciting area of research and, as often happens in science, the first stage brings amazing and novel results. In the second stage, further studies take into account and examine additional variables in order to develop more comprehensive theories. The challenge for the next generation of embodied cognition researchers is to examine these moderating variables and develop a theory that explains how, when, and why these fascinating associations between body and mind occur.

Future studies could examine, for instance, when physical sensations have the least influence. For example, we learned that touching a warm object influences our judgements and behaviour, but outdoor temperatures might influence this association – touching a warm object may have a different effect on a cold day as compared with a hot day. Other factors, such as the presence of other people, might also affect the association between physical sensation and behaviour. Future studies should also include a diversity of cultures and children of various ages to better understand the scaffolding process by which the association between concrete and abstract concepts occurs.

The association between physical sensations, behaviours and emotions might also be stronger for certain types of individuals than for others. Some people tend to be more responsive to environmental cues and evince a high sensitivity to physical sensations. Some are more sensitive than others and more preoccupied with their bodies. It is logical to assume that such people will be more influenced by physical sensations than those who are less sensitive to the same cues. We can also become more attuned to our bodies through the practice of yoga or meditation. When I started taking yoga classes, I became more aware of my body and my breathing, and also was able to notice the environment around me more acutely.

I would like to see more studies employ new technologies, such as functional magnetic resonance imaging, in order to view the machinery of the mind – the brain – in action, to map brain activities related to speech and action and help further confirm the links between the body and the mind.

Another way to expand the findings is to investigate the myriad influences of virtual reality that we are increasingly exposed to. Nowadays more and more activities take place in the virtual environment as we sit in rooms, sometimes without much light, gazing at the screens of our computers, tablet computers, or smartphones. A growing proportion of our social and financial activities takes place in virtual environments, a trend that is only rising. Increasingly, our retail purchases are made online, while physical visits to the bank are becoming less and less necessary as we execute financial transactions online. These changes hold true not only for financial activities but also for our social activities. Today we interact via social networks such as Facebook, dating websites, and various social, support and discussion groups, all via the Internet. Future studies need to investigate how the physical dimensions of these virtual environments influence our decisions, behaviours and emotions.

Take banks, for example. The bank presents various options for investments, savings and loans, and it uses physical characteristics, such as color and vertical positioning, to influence our decisions. When a bank wants to interest you in a particular loan or investment, it might present the information in a poster that depicts a floating balloon or a heavy metal lockbox or safe. Such a weight-related cue can work both ways. If the bank offer is for an investment, then the depiction of weight influences us to believe it is safe and sure. An investment offer depicted as floating away on a balloon is unlikely to be persuasive. An offer concerning a loan that will not weigh us down but allow us to float towards a goal might influence us to take it seriously, while a heavy image for a loan could put us off.

Our virtual environments also alter our physical behaviour. For example, we enlarge the letters on our digital tablets and iPhone screens by touching the screen with two fingers of one hand and moving them apart. The growing universality of this action might create a new representation of the concepts of large and small. Just recently I saw a child looking at a book and making this movement above the page in order to try to enlarge the picture; she was surprised when her action had no effect.

We've only just begun to understand the tantalising web of embodied connections that plug us into our environments. This book is a modest attempt to build upon this knowledge and open new roads into yet undiscovered territory. The findings have important implications and can help us in both our professional and our personal lives. We may use what we have learned from these studies in our interactions with our spouses, children, friends, co-workers and bosses; and for negotiations, job interviews, first dates and important talks with family members or our children's teachers.

The beauty of these findings is that they apply to virtually everyone. Once you become aware of these influences and the power of metaphors, you can use them for your benefit. As you've learned, some are positive and helpful, but some can be misleading. Sweet-loving people can be kinder than others, for instance, but not all clean, bright, powerful people whom we look up to are worthy of our trust. Pay attention to your senses' input and evaluate it. Your attunement to what your senses tell you will give you physical intelligence – otherwise, your senses will yield only data. Armed with this new awareness, you may avoid being swayed by previously unconscious metaphorical associations in your judgements and evaluations of others.

With new awareness of these associations, you'll find that you pay more attention to environmental factors, such as colour, temperature and texture. You can see them with new eyes. You can even speak a new language – that of embodied metaphor. I hope that this new physical intelligence will add to your enjoyment of life.

Environmental cues are everywhere. And you are now equipped to explore them further with your new physical intelligence.

Acknowledgements

I have always wanted to write a book for the general public that would help people better understand what influences our behaviour, thoughts and emotions. For 30 years I have conducted and published studies in scientific journals, but writing this book was a totally different journey that I could not have completed without the help of a number of people.

I am deeply indebted to my agent, Lindsay Edgecombe, of the Levine Greenberg Literary Agency. She is the best literary agent a writer could ever hope to work with. Talented, extremely smart and perceptive, Lindsay offered the most valuable suggestions. This book would not have been possible without her guidance and assistance. She saw the potential in my proposal, believed in this book, fine-tuned its focus, and directed me every step of the way.

My editor at Atria, Leslie Meredith, believed in the book when she first saw the proposal, and her editorial input was enormously helpful. Leslie is a great editor with a sharp, critical eye. With her excellent editorial skills, insightful comments and suggestions, she improved the book tremendously and gave it its final polish. I also thank Donna Loffredo, the associate editor; Ariele Fredman, my publicist; and the fine staff at Simon & Schuster who helped in so many different ways.

David Angeloff and Ben Ehrlich made invaluable contributions to the book. They are both extremely talented and intelligent, and offered insightful and valuable suggestions as well as comments that sharpened the writing. Thank you, David and Ben.

I was fortunate to have two terrific students, Lior Kalay-Shahin and Allon Cohen. They are the best students a professor could ever wish for – talented, intelligent, creative and enthusiastic. The three of us became a team and held countless lengthy discussions about the ideas and studies presented in this book. Lior helped me in so many different ways, read the book, and offered extremely valuable feedback. Both Lior and Allon brought creativity and joy into our work. Thank you both.

Ofri Katz, Harvey Frenkiel, Nina Davis, Uri Yariv and Danny Yagil helped in many different ways.

I wish to thank the researchers who conducted many of the creative and interesting studies I report in the book. I have met some of them and have corresponded with others, or have simply read their work. I also wish to thank the many students who took my courses in recent years and contributed their insights and suggestions.

I am grateful to my late parents, Dora and Hillel Jacobson. My mother inspired me; she always encouraged me to follow my dreams and conveyed this message very clearly. My father was forever supportive of me in every possible way.

Special thanks to my friends Ruli Arnon, Irit Shavit, Debbie Morag, Anat Savidor and Nira Preiskel. Loyal and close to my heart, all were keenly interested in the process of writing this book. I also wish to thank my colleagues and friends who worked with me for years and were always a source of support – Yona Teichman, Amiram Raviv, Danny Algom and Dov Shmotkin.

I want to conclude with the most important people in my life, my family, for their unwavering support. My amazing children Orly and Dory encouraged me to fulfil my dream to write this book, and provided advice when I needed it. Each of them has achieved greatness and success in their respective careers while managing to raise beautiful families. They inspire me and are a continuous influence and light in my life. While I was writing this book, I often imagined what my son Dani would have said about various ideas.

My son-in-law On Amir, my daughter-in-law Keren Kohen-Lobel, my brother Raffi Jacobson and his partner Rick Sylvester were always wonderfully supportive.

My granddaughters Danielle, Elinor, Natalie and Dean are endless sources of joy. Their childlike innocence and sense of wonder motivates me to write and explore.

Last but not least, I want to thank my husband, David Lobel, for always believing in me, supporting me, and being there for me. For understanding my passion for my work, for tolerating and never complaining about the long hours I spent in front of the computer – including the times I should have been relaxing with him. Thank you, David.

Thalma Lobel
December 2013

Notes

Introduction: The Tangled Web Our Senses Weave

1. L.E. Williams and J.A. Bargh (2008). Experiencing physical warmth promotes interpersonal warmth. *Science, 322* (5901), 606–7.

Chapter 1. Wanna Grab a Drink? How Temperature Affects Us

1. L.E. Williams and J.A. Bargh (2008). Experiencing physical warmth promotes interpersonal warmth. *Science, 322* (5901), 606–7.
2. H. Ijzerman and G.R. Semin (2009). The thermometer of social relations: Mapping social proximity on temperature. *Psychological Science, 20* (10), 1214–20.
3. L.W. Barsalou (2008). Grounded cognition. *Annual Review of Psychology, 59*, 617–45; R.W. Gibbs (1992). Categorization and metaphor understanding. *Psychological Review, 99* (3), 572–77; P.M. Niedenthal, L.W. Barsalou, P. Winkielman, S. Krauth-Gruber, and F. Ric (2005). Embodiment in attitudes, social perception, and emotion. *Personality and Social Psychology Review, 9* (3), 184–211; M. Wilson (2002). Six views of embodied cognition. *Psychonomic Bulletin & Review, 9* (4), 625–36.
4. L.E. Williams, J.Y. Huang, and J.A. Bargh (2009). The scaffolded mind: Higher mental processes are grounded in early experience of the physical world. *European Journal of Social Psychology, 39* (7), 1257–67; G. Lakoff and M. Johnson (1999). *Philosophy in the flesh: The embodied mind and its challenge to Western thought.* New York: Basic Books; M.J. Landau, B.P. Meier, and L.A. Keefer (2010). A metaphor-enriched social cognition. *Psychological Bulletin, 136* (6), 1045–67.

5. M.R. Cunningham (1979). Weather, mood, and helping behavior: Quasi experiments with the sunshine Samaritan. *Journal of Personality and Social Psychology, 37* (11), 1947–56.

6. E.G. Cohn and J. Rotton (2005). The curve is still out there: A reply to Bushman, Wang, and Anderson's (2005) 'Is the curve relating temperature to aggression linear or curvilinear?' *Journal of Personality and Social Psychology, 89* (1), 67–70; J. Rotton and E.G. Cohn (2004). Outdoor temperature, climate control and criminal assault: The spatial and temporal ecology of violence. *Environment and Behavior, 36* (2), 276–306; C.A. Anderson (1987). Temperature and aggression: Effects on quarterly, yearly, and city rates of violent and nonviolent crime. *Journal of Personality and Social Psychology, 52* (6), 1161–73.

7. C.B. Zhong and G.J. Leonardelli (2008). Cold and lonely: Does social exclusion literally feel cold? *Psychological Science, 19* (9), 838–42.

8. H. Ijzerman, M. Gallucci, W.T. Pouw, S.C. Weißgerber, N.J. Van Doesum, and K.D. Williams (2012). Cold-blooded loneliness: Social exclusion leads to lower skin temperatures. *Acta Psychologica, 140* (3), 283–88.

9. Williams and Bargh. Experiencing physical warmth promotes interpersonal warmth.

10. Y. Kang, L.E. Williams, M.S. Clark, J.R. Gray, and J.A. Bargh (2011). Physical temperature effects on trust behavior: The role of insula. *Social Cognitive and Affective Neuroscience, 6* (4), 507–15.

Chapter 2. Smooth Operators and Rough Customers: Texture

1. T. Field (2002). Infants' need for touch. *Human Development, 45* (2), 100–3.

2. J. Hornik (1992). Tactile stimulation and consumer response. *Journal of Consumer Research, 19* (3), 449–58.

3. J. Levav and J.J. Argo (2010). Physical contact and financial risk taking. *Psychological Science, 21* (6), 804.

4. A.H. Crusco and C.G. Wetzel (1984). The Midas touch: The effects of interpersonal touch on restaurant tipping. *Personality and Social Psychology Bulletin, 10* (4), 512–17.

5. J. Cha, M. Eid, L. Rahal, and A. El Saddik (2008). HugMe: An interpersonal haptic communication system. *IEEE International Workshop on Haptic Audio Visual Environments and Games, 2008,* 99–102.

6. J. Teh, S.P. Lee, and A.D. Cheok (2005). Internet pajama: A mobile hugging communication system. *Proceedings of the 2005 International Conference on Augmented Tele-Existence,* 274.

7. J.M. Ackerman, C.C. Nocera, and J.A. Bargh (2010). Incidental haptic sensations influence social judgments and decisions. *Science, 328* (5986), 1712–15.

8. M.L. Slepian, M. Weisbuch, N.O. Rule, and N. Ambady (2011). Tough and tender: Embodied categorization of gender. *Psychological Science, 22* (1), 26–28.

9. D. Hayes (2005). Candidate qualities through a partisan lens: A theory of trait ownership. *American Journal of Political Science, 49* (4), 908–23.

10. M.L. Slepian, N.O. Rule, and N. Ambady (2012). Proprioception and person perception: Politicians and professors. *Personality and Social Psychology Bulletin, 39* (12), 1621–28.

11. Ackerman, Nocera, and Bargh. Incidental haptic sensations influence social judgments and decisions.
12. S. Lacey, R. Stilla, and K. Sathian (2012). Metaphorically feeling: Comprehending textural metaphors activates somatosensory cortex. *Brain and Language, 120 (3)*, 416–21.
13. J. Nimer and B. Lundahl (2007). Animal-assisted therapy: A meta-analysis. *Anthrozoos: A Multidisciplinary Journal of the Interactions of People and Animals, 20 (3)*, 225–38.
14. M.M. Baun and B.W. McCabe (2003). Companion animals and persons with dementia of the Alzheimer's type. *American Behavioral Scientist, 47 (1)*, 42–51; J.M. Grossberg and E.F. Alf (1985). Interaction with pet dogs: Effects on human cardiovascular response. *Journal of the Delta Society, 2 (1)*, 20–27.

Chapter 3. Don't Take This Lightly: The Importance of Weight

1. J.M. Ackerman, C.C. Nocera, and J.A. Bargh (2010). Incidental haptic sensations influence social judgments and decisions. *Science, 328* (5986), 1712–15.
2. F. Pratto, L.M. Stallworth, and J. Sidanius (1997). The gender gap: Differences in political attitudes and social dominance orientation. *British Journal of Social Psychology, 36* (1), 49–68; A.B. Diekman, A.H. Eagly, and P. Kulesa (2002). Accuracy and bias in stereotypes about the social and political attitudes of women and men. *Journal of Experimental Social Psychology, 38* (3), 268–82.
3. N.B. Jostmann, D. Lakens, and T.W. Schubert (2009). Weight as an embodiment of importance. *Psychological Science, 20* (9), 1169–74.
4. I.K. Schneider, B.T. Rutjens, N.B. Jostmann, and D. Lakens (2011). Weighty matters: Importance literally feels heavy. *Social Psychological and Personality Science, 2* (5), 474–78.
5. M.L. Slepian, E.J. Masicampo, N.R. Toosi, and N. Ambady (2012). The physical burdens of secrecy. *Journal of Experimental Psychology: General, 141* (4), 619–24.
6. D.R. Proffitt, J. Stefanucci, T. Banton, and W. Epstein (2003). The role of effort in perceiving distance. *Psychological Science, 14* (2), 106–12.

Chapter 4. Slow Down, Red Ahead: Red and Performance

1. For example: M. Shih, T.L. Pittinsky, and N. Ambady (1999). Stereotype susceptibility: Identity salience and shifts in quantitative performance. *Psychological Science, 10* (1), 80–83.
2. For example: C.M. Steele and J. Aronson (1995). Stereotype threat and the intellectual test performance of African Americans. *Journal of Personality and Social Psychology, 69* (5), 797–811.
3. A.J. Elliot, M.A. Maier, A.C. Moller, R. Friedman, and J. Meinhardt (2007). Color and psychological functioning: The effect of red on performance attainment. *Journal of Experimental Psychology: General, 136* (1), 154–68.
4. A.J. Elliot, M.A. Maier, M.J. Binser, R. Friedman, and R. Pekrun (2009). The

effect of red on avoidance behavior in achievement contexts. *Personality and Social Psychology Bulletin, 35* (3), 365–75.

5. R.A. Hill and R.A. Barton (2005). Red enhances human performance in contests. *Nature, 435* (7040), 293.

6. M.J. Attrill, K.A. Gresty, R.A. Hill, and R.A. Barton (2008). Red shirt colour is associated with long-term team success in English football. *Journal of Sports Sciences, 26* (6), 577–82.

7. N. Hagemann, B. Strauss, and J. Leißing (2008). When the referee sees red. *Psychological Science, 19* (8), 769–71.

8. A.J. Elliot and H. Aarts (2011). Perception of the color red enhances the force and velocity of motor output. *Emotion, 11* (2), 445–49.

9. A. Ilie, S. Ioan, L. Zagrean, and M. Moldovan (2008). Better to be red than blue in virtual competition. *CyberPsychology and Behavior, 11* (3), 375–77.

Chapter 5. The Lady in Red: Red and Sexual Attraction

1. A.J. Elliot and D. Niesta (2008). Romantic red: Red enhances men's attraction to women. *Journal of Personality and Social Psychology, 95* (5), 1150–64.

2. A.J. Elliot, J.L. Tracy, A.D. Pazda, and A.T. Beall (2012). Red enhances women's attractiveness to men: First evidence suggesting universality. *Journal of Experimental Social Psychology, 49* (1), 165–68.

3. D. Niesta Kayser, A.J. Elliot, and R. Feltman (2010). Red and romantic behavior in men viewing women. *European Journal of Social Psychology, 40* (6), 901–8.

4. N. Guéguen and C. Jacob (2012). Clothing color and tipping: Gentlemen patrons give more tips to waitresses with red clothes. *Journal of Hospitality and Tourism Research*, April 18, 2012.

5. N. Guéguen (2012). Color and women hitchhikers' attractiveness: Gentlemen drivers preferred. *Color Research and Application, 37* (1), 76–78.

6. C. Waitt, M.S. Gerald, A.C. Little, and E. Kraiselburd (2006). Selective attention toward female secondary sexual color in male rhesus macaques. *American Journal of Primatology, 68* (7), 738–44.

7. J.M. Setchell and E.J. Wickings (2005). Dominance, status signals and coloration in male mandrills (*Mandrillus sphinx*). *Ethology, 111* (1), 25–50.

8. S.R. Pryke and S.C. Griffith (2006). Red dominates black: Agonistic signalling among head morphs in the colour polymorphic Gouldian finch. *Proceedings of the Royal Society of London. Series B: Biological Sciences, 273* (1589), 949–57.

9. I.C. Cuthill, S. Hunt, C. Cleary, and C. Clark (1997). Colour bands, dominance, and body mass regulation in male zebra finches (*Taeniopygia guttata*). *Proceedings of the Royal Society of London. Series B: Biological Sciences, 264* (1384), 1093–99.

10. T.C. Bakker and M. Milinski (1993). The advantages of being red: Sexual selection in the stickleback. *Marine and Freshwater Behaviour and Physiology, 23* (1–4), 287–300.

11. A.C. Little and R.A. Hill (2007). Attribution to red suggests special role in dominance signalling. *Journal of Evolutionary Psychology, 5* (1–4), 161–68.

12. A.J. Elliot, D. Niesta Kayser, T. Greitemeyer, S. Lichtenfeld, R.H. Gramzow, M.A. Maier, and H. Liu (2010). Red, rank, and romance in women viewing men. *Journal of Experimental Psychology: General, 139* (3), 399–417.

13. N.M. Puccinelli, R. Chandrashekaran, D. Grewal, and R. Suri (2013). Are men seduced by red? The effect of red versus black prices on price perceptions. *Journal of Retailing, 89* (2), 115–25.

14. T.L. Morris, J. Gorham, S.H. Cohen, and D. Huffman (1996). Fashion in the classroom: Effects of attire on student perceptions of instructors in college classes. *Communication Education, 45* (2), 135–48.

15. P. Glick, S. Larsen, C. Johnson, and H. Branstiter (2005). Evaluations of sexy women in low- and high-status jobs. *Psychology of Women Quarterly, 29* (4), 389–95.

16. C.Y. Shao, J. Baker, and J.A. Wagner (2004). The effects of appropriateness of service contact personnel dress on customer expectations of service quality and purchase intention: The moderating influences of involvement and gender. *Journal of Business Research, 57* (10), 1164–76.

17. H. Adam and A.D. Galinsky (2012). Enclothed cognition. *Journal of Experimental Social Psychology, 48* (4), 918–25.

Chapter 6. In Contrast: Separating the Light from the Darkness

1. B.P. Meier, M.D. Robinson, and G.L. Clore (2004). Why good guys wear white: Automatic inferences about stimulus valence based on brightness. *Psychological Science, 15* (2), 82–87.

2. D. Lakens, G.R. Semin, and F. Foroni (2011). But for the bad, there would not be good: Grounding valence in brightness through shared relational structures. *Journal of Experimental Psychology: General, 141* (3), 584–94.

3. M.G. Frank and T. Gilovich (1988). The dark side of self- and social perception: Black uniforms and aggression in professional sports. *Journal of Personality and Social Psychology, 54* (1), 74–85.

4. G.D. Webster, G.R. Urland, and J. Correll (2012). Can uniform color color aggression? Quasi-experimental evidence from professional ice hockey. *Social Psychological and Personality Science, 3* (3), 274–81.

5. B.P. Meier, M.D. Robinson, L.E. Crawford, and W.J. Ahlvers (2007). When 'light' and 'dark' thoughts become light and dark responses: Affect biases brightness judgments. *Emotion, 7* (2), 366–76.

6. H. Song, A.J. Vonasch, B.P. Meier, and J.A. Bargh (2012). Brighten up: Smiles facilitate perceptual judgment of facial lightness. *Journal of Experimental Social Psychology, 48* (1), 450–52.

7. P. Banerjee, P. Chatterjee, and J. Sinha (2012). Is it light or dark? Recalling moral behavior changes perception of brightness. *Psychological Science, 23* (4), 407–9.

8. G.D. Sherman and G.L. Clore (2009). The color of sin: White and black are perceptual symbols of moral purity and pollution. *Psychological Science, 20* (8), 1019–25.

9. C. Zhong, V.K. Bohns, and F. Gino (2010). Good lamps are the best police: Darkness increases dishonesty and self-interested behavior. *Psychological Science, 21* (3), 311–14.

10. M. aan het Rot, D.S. Moskowitz, and S.N. Young. (2008). Exposure to bright light is associated with positive social interaction and good mood over short time periods: A naturalistic study in mildly seasonal people. *Journal of Psychiatric Research, 42* (4), 311–19.

11. S. Leppämäki, T. Partonen, P. Piiroinen, J. Haukka, and J. Lönnqvist (2003). Timed bright-light exposure and complaints related to shift work among women. *Scandinavian Journal of Work, Environment and Health, 29* (1), 22–26.

Chapter 7. Space, the Mental Frontier: Physical and Psychological Distance

1. L. Festinger, S. Schachter, and K. Back (1950). *Social pressures in informal groups: A study of human factors in housing.* Oxford, England: Harper.
2. D.P. Kennedy, J. Gläscher, J.M. Tyszka, & R. Adolphs (2009). Personal space regulation by the human amygdala. *Nature Neuroscience, 12* (10), 1226[0].
3. J. Xu, H. Shen, and R.S. Wyer (2012). Does the distance between us matter? Influences of physical proximity to others on consumer choice. *Journal of Consumer Psychology, 22* (3), 418–23.
4. J. Mumm and B. Mutlu (2011). Human-robot proxemics: Physical and psychological distancing in human-robot interaction. *2011 Sixth ACM/IEEE International Conference on Human-Robot Interaction,* 331–38.
5. A. Galin, M. Gross, and G. Gosalker (2007). E-negotiation versus face-to-face negotiation: What has changed – if anything? *Computers in Human Behavior, 23* (1), 787–97.
6. L.E. Williams and J.A. Bargh (2008). Keeping one's distance: The influence of spatial distance cues on affect and evaluation. *Psychological Science, 19* (3), 302–8.
7. E.M. Sahlstein (2004). Relating at a distance: Negotiating being together and being apart in long-distance relationships. *Journal of Social and Personal Relationships, 21* (5), 689–710.

Chapter 8. High and Mighty: Vertical Position, Size and Power

1. T.W. Schubert (2005). Your highness: Vertical positions as perceptual symbols of power. *Journal of Personality and Social Psychology, 89* (1), 1–21.
2. K. Zanolie, S. v. Dantzig, I. Boot, J. Wijnen, T.W. Schubert, S.R. Giessner, and D. Pecher (2012). Mighty metaphors: Behavioral and ERP evidence that power shifts attention on a vertical dimension. *Brain and Cognition, 78* (1), 50–58.
3. T.W. Schubert. Your highness: Vertical positions as perceptual symbols of power. *Journal of Personality and Social Psychology, 89* (1), 1–21.
4. S.R. Giessner and T.W. Schubert (2007). High in the hierarchy: How vertical location and judgments of leaders' power are interrelated. *Organizational Behavior and Human Decision Processes, 104* (1), 30–44.
5. P.A. Higham and D.W. Carment. (1992). The rise and fall of politicians: The judged heights of Broadbent, Mulroney and Turner before and after the 1988 Canadian federal election. *Canadian Journal of Behavioural Science/Revue Canadienne des Sciences du Comportement, 24* (3), 404–9.
6. S.R. Giessner and T.W. Schubert (2007). High in the hierarchy: How vertical location and judgments of leaders' power are interrelated. *Organizational Behavior and Human Decision Processes, 104* (1), 30–44.
7. V. Carrieri and M. De Paola (2012). Height and subjective well-being in Italy. *Economics and Human Biology, 10* (3), 289–98.

8. T.A. Judge and D.M. Cable (2004). The effect of physical height on workplace success and income: Preliminary test of a theoretical model. *Journal of Applied Psychology, 89* (3), 428–40.

9. A.J. Yap, M.F. Mason, and D.R. Ames (2012). The powerful size others down: The link between power and estimates of others' size. *Journal of Experimental Social Psychology. 49 (3)*, 591–94.

10. M.M. Duguid and J.A. Goncalo (2012). Living large. *Psychological Science, 23* (1), 36–40.

11. S.R. Giessner, M.K. Ryan, T.W. Schubert, and N. van Quaquebeke (2011). The power of pictures: Vertical picture angles in power pictures. *Media Psychology, 14* (4), 442–64.

12. B.P. Meier and S. Dionne. (2009). Downright sexy: Verticality, implicit power, and perceived physical attractiveness. *Social Cognition, 27* (6), 883–92.

13. Giessner, Ryan, Schubert, and van Quaquebeke. The power of pictures.

14. B.P. Meier and M.D. Robinson (2004). Why the sunny side is up: Associations between affect and vertical position. *Psychological Science, 15* (4), 243–47.

15. B.P. Meier, D.J. Hauser, M.D. Robinson, C.K. Friesen, and K. Schjeldahl (2007). What's 'up' with God? Vertical space as a representation of the divine. *Journal of Personality and Social Psychology, 93* (5), 699–710.

16. E.L. Brainerd (1994). Pufferfish inflation: Functional morphology of postcranial structures in *Diodon holocanthus* (Tetraodontiformes). *Journal of Morphology, 220* (3), 243–61.

17. L.F. Toledo, I. Sazima, and C.F. Haddad (2011). Behavioural defences of anurans: An overview. *Ethology Ecology and Evolution, 23* (1), 1–25.

18. H.W. Greene (1988). Antipredator mechanisms in reptiles, 1–152 In: C. Gans and R.B. Huey (eds.), *Biology of the Reptilia*, Vol. 16, *Ecology B, Defense and life history*. New York: Alan R. Liss.

19. D. Goodwin (1956). Further observations on the behaviour of the jay Garrulus glandarius. *Ibis, 98* (2), 186–219.

20. F. De Waal (2007). Chimpanzee politics: Power and sex among apes. Baltimore, MD: Johns Hopkins University Press.

21. T.W. Schubert, S. Waldzus, and S.R. Giessner (2009). Control over the association of power and size. *Social Cognition, 27* (1), 1–19.

22. D. Dubois, D.D. Rucker, and A.D. Galinsky (2012). Super size me: Product as a signal of status. *Journal of Consumer Research, 38* (6), 1047–62.

23. D.R. Carney, A.J.C. Cuddy, and A.J. Yap (2010). Power posing. *Psychological Science, 21* (10), 1363–68.

Chapter 9. Out, Damned Spot: Guilt, Morality and Cleaning

1. C.B. Zhong and K. Liljenquist (2006). Washing away your sins: Threatened morality and physical cleansing. *Science, 313* (5792), 1451–52.

2. N. Fairbrother, S.J. Newth, and S. Rachman (2005). Mental pollution: Feelings of dirtiness without physical contact. *Behaviour Research and Therapy, 43* (1), 121–30.

3. V. Lee (2012). Hell du jour: Meet Israel's daylight prostitutes. *Haaretz*, October 11, http://www.haaretz.com/weekend/magazine/hell-du-jour-meet-israels-daylight-prostitutes-1.469461.

4.   S.W.S. Lee and N. Schwarz (2010). Dirty hands and dirty mouths: Embodi-
     ment of the moral-purity metaphor is specific to the motor modality involved
     in moral transgression. *Psychological Science, 21* (10), 1423–25.
5.   Zhong and Liljenquist. Washing away your sins.
6.   H.A. Chapman, D.A. Kim, J.M. Susskind, and A.K. Anderson (2009). In bad
     taste: Evidence for the oral origins of moral disgust. *Science, 323* (5918), 1222–26.
7.   S. Schnall, J. Haidt, G.L. Clore, and A.H. Jordan (2008). Disgust as embodied
     moral judgment. *Personality and Social Psychology Bulletin, 34* (8), 1096–1109.
8.   K.J. Eskine, N.A. Kacinik, and J.J. Prinz (2011). A bad taste in the mouth:
     Gustatory disgust influences moral judgment. *Psychological Science, 22* (3),
     295–99.
9.   S. Schnall, J. Benton, and S. Harvey (2008). With a clean conscience: Clean-
     liness reduces the severity of moral judgments. *Psychological Science, 19* (12),
     1219–22.
10. Ibid.
11. C. Zhong, B. Strejcek, and N. Sivanathan (2010). A clean self can render
     harsh moral judgment. *Journal of Experimental Social Psychology, 46* (5),
     859–62.
12. S.W.S. Lee and N. Schwarz (2010). Washing away postdecisional dissonance.
     Science, 328 (5979), 709.
13. A.J. Xu, R. Zwick, and N. Schwarz (2012). Washing away your (good or bad)
     luck: Physical cleansing affects risk-taking behavior. *Journal of Experimental
     Psychology: General, 141* (1), 26–30.

Chapter 10. Sweet Smell of Success: Taste and Smell

1.   B.P. Meier, S.K. Moeller, M. Riemer-Peltz, and M.D. Robinson (2012). Sweet
     taste preferences and experiences predict prosocial inferences, personalities, and
     behaviors. *Journal of Personality and Social Psychology, 102* (1), 163–74.
2.   C.B. Zhong and S.E. DeVoe (2010). You are how you eat: Fast food and
     impatience. *Psychological Science, 21* (5), 619–22.
3.   L. Douce and W. Janssens (2013). The presence of a pleasant ambient scent
     in a fashion store: The moderating role of shopping motivation and affect
     intensity. *Environment and Behavior, 45* (2), 215–38.
4.   J. Chebat, M. Morrin, and D. Chebat (2009). Does age attenuate the impact
     of pleasant ambient scent on consumer response? *Environment and Behavior,
     41* (2), 258–67.
5.   E.R. Spangenberg, A.E. Crowley, and P.W. Henderson (1996). Improving the
     store environment: Do olfactory cues affect evaluations and behaviors? *Journal
     of Marketing, 60* (2), 67–80.
6.   K. Ravn (2007). Smells like sales. *Los Angeles Times,* August 20, F-1.
7.   A.R. Hirsch (1995). Effects of ambient odors on slot-machine usage in a Las
     Vegas casino. *Psychology and Marketing, 12* (7), 585–94.
8.   N. Guéguen and C. Petr (2006). Odors and consumer behavior in a restau-
     rant. *International Journal of Hospitality Management, 25* (2), 335–39.
9.   H.N. Schifferstein, K.S. Talke, and D. Oudshoorn (2011). Can ambient scent
     enhance the nightlife experience? *Chemosensory Perception, 4* (1–2), 55–64.
10. M. Moss, S. Hewitt, L. Moss, and K. Wesnes (2008). Modulation of cog-
     nitive performance and mood by aromas of peppermint and ylang-ylang.

International Journal of Neuroscience, 118 (1), 59–77; P.R. Zoladz and B. Raudenbush (2005). Cognitive enhancement through stimulation of the chemical senses. *North American Journal of Psychology, 7* (1), 125–38; S. Barker, P. Grayhem, J. Koon, J. Perkins, A. Whalen, and B. Raudenbush (2003). Improved performance on clerical tasks associated with administration of peppermint odor. *Perceptual and Motor Skills, 97* (3), 1007–10; K. McCombs, B. Raudenbush, A. Bova, and M. Sappington (2011). Effects of peppermint scent administration on cognitive video game performance. *North American Journal of Psychology, 13* (3), 383–90.

11. B. Raudenbush (2000). The effects of odors on objective and subjective measures of physical performance. *Aroma-Chology Review, 9* (1), 1–5.

12. B. Raudenbush, N. Corley, and W. Eppich (2001). Enhancing athletic performance through the administration of peppermint odor. *Journal of Sport and Exercise Psychology, 23* (2), 156–60.

13. R.A. Baron (1997). The sweet smell of . . . helping: Effects of pleasant ambient fragrance on prosocial behavior in shopping malls. *Personality and Social Psychology Bulletin, 23* (5), 498–503.

14. N. Guéguen (2012). The sweet smell of . . . courtship: Effects of pleasant ambient fragrance on women's receptivity to a man's courtship request. *Journal of Environmental Psychology, 32* (2), 123–25.

15. D.M. Zemke and S. Shoemaker (2008). A sociable atmosphere: Ambient scent's effect on social interaction. *Cornell Hospitality Quarterly, 49* (3), 317–29.

16. R.W. Holland, M. Hendriks, and H. Aarts (2005). Smells like clean spirit: Nonconscious effects of scent on cognition and behavior. *Psychological Science, 16* (9), 689–93.

17. S.W. Lee and N. Schwarz (2012). Bidirectionality, mediation, and moderation of metaphorical effects: The embodiment of social suspicion and fishy smells. *Journal of Personality and Social Psychology, 103* (5), 737–49.

Chapter 11. Turning on Lights Outside the Box: Embodying Metaphors

1. X. Li, L. Wei, and D. Soman (2010). Sealing the emotions genie: The effects of physical enclosure on psychological closure. *Psychological Science, 21* (8), 1047–50.

2. A.K. Leung, S. Kim, E. Polman, L.S. Ong, L. Qiu, J.A. Goncalo, and J. Sanchez-Burks (2012). Embodied metaphors and creative 'acts'. *Psychological Science, 23* (5), 502–9.

3. S. Mednick (1962). The associative basis of the creative process. *Psychological Review, 69* (3), 220–32.

4. J.J. Ratey (2010). *Spark! The revolutionary new science of exercise and the brain.* London: Quercus Books.

5. M.L. Slepian, M. Weisbuch, A.M. Rutchick, L.S. Newman, and N. Ambady (2010). Shedding light on insight: Priming bright ideas. *Journal of Experimental Social Psychology, 46* (4), 696–700.

6. G.M. Fitzsimons, T.L. Chartrand, and G.J. Fitzsimons (2008). Automatic effects of brand exposure on motivated behavior: How Apple makes you 'think different'. *Journal of Consumer Research, 35* (1), 21–35.

7. E.B. Gurman (1989). Travel abroad: A way to increase creativity? *Educational Research Quarterly, 13* (3), 12–16.

Index